WOMEN IN CRIMINAL JUSTICE

METROPOLITAN COLLEGE
OF NEW YORK LIBRARY
75 Varick Street 12th Fl.
New York, NY 10013

WOMEN IN CRIMINAL JUSTICE

VONCILE B. GOWDY, TRAVIS CAIN,
RICHARD SUTTON, ET AL.

Novinka Books
New York

Senior Editors: Susan Boriotti and Donna Dennis
Coordinating Editor: Tatiana Shohov
Office Manager: Annette Hellinger
Graphics: Wanda Serrano
Editorial Production: Marius Andronie, Maya Columbus, Vladimir Klestov,
Matthew Kozlowski, Tom Moceri and Anthony T. Sovak
Circulation: Ave Maria Gonzalez, Vera Popovic, Luis Aviles, Raymond Davis,
Melissa Diaz, Magdalene Nunez, Marlene Nunez and Jeannie Pappas
Communications and Acquisitions: Serge P. Shohov
Marketing: Cathy DeGregory

Library of Congress Cataloging-in-Publication Data

Gowdy, Voncile B.
  Women in criminal justice / Voncile B. Gowdy, Travis Cain, Richard Sutton, et al.
    p. cm.
"An update of The report of the LEAA [Law Enforcement Assistance Administration] Task Force on Women, published in October 1974"--Pref.
  ISBN: 1-59033-736-0 (softcover)
1. Sex discrimination in criminal justice administration—United States. 2. Female offenders—United States. 3. Female juvenile delinquents—United States. 4. Women—Crimes against—United States. 5. Women criminal justice personnel—United States. I. Cain, Travis. II. Sutton, Richard C., 1951- III. United States. Law Enforcement Assistance Administration. Task Force on Women. Report of the LEAA Task Force on Women. IV. Title.

HV9950.G69 2003
364'.082'0973—dc21

2003008967

Copyright © 2003 by Novinka Books, An Imprint of
  Nova Science Publishers, Inc.
  400 Oser Ave, Suite 1600
  Hauppauge, New York 11788-3619
  Tele. 631-231-7269   Fax 631-231-8175
  e-mail: Novascience@earthlink.net
  Web Site: http://www.novapublishers.com

All rights reserved. No part of this book may be reproduced, stored in a retrieval system or transmitted in any form or by any means: electronic, electrostatic, magnetic, tape, mechanical photocopying, recording or otherwise without permission from the publishers.

The authors and publisher have taken care in preparation of this book, but make no expressed or implied warranty of any kind and assume no responsibility for any errors or omissions. No liability is assumed for incidental or consequential damages in connection with or arising out of information contained in this book.

This publication is designed to provide accurate and authoritative information with regard to the subject matter covered herein. It is sold with the clear understanding that the publisher is not engaged in rendering legal or any other professional services. If legal or any other expert assistance is required, the services of a competent person should be sought. FROM A DECLARATION OF PARTICIPANTS JOINTLY ADOPTED BY A COMMITTEE OF THE AMERICAN BAR ASSOCIATION AND A COMMITTEE OF PUBLISHERS.

Printed in the United States of America

Contents

Contributors		vii
Introduction		ix
Executive Summary		xi
Chapter 1	Adult Female Offenders	1
Chapter 2	Female Juvenile Offenders	19
Chapter 3	Women and Girls as Victims	43
Chapter 4	Women Who Work in the Criminal Justice System	67
Conclusion		83
Index		85

CONTRIBUTORS

The team that developed this report includes the following:

Dr. Voncile B. Gowdy
Chair, OJP Coordination Group on Women
National Institute of Justice

Travis Cain
Office of Juvenile Justice and
Delinquency Prevention

The Honorable Helen Corrothers[*]
Visiting Fellow
National Institute of Justice

Teresa Hunt Katsel
Federal Bureau of Prisons

Angela Moore Parmley
National Institute of Justice

Annesley Schmidt
Federal Bureau of Prisons

Dr. Richard Sutton
Bureau of Justice Assistance

---

[*] Individuals noted with an asterisk no longer work for the U.S. Department of Justice.

Andie Moss
National Institute of Corrections

Alethea Camp[*]
National Institute of Corrections

Sharon English[*]
Office for Victims of Crime

Jody Zepp[*]
National Institute of Corrections

Additionally, the authors would like to acknowledge the assistance of the following individuals:

Tracy Snell
Bureau of Justice Statistics

Doug Roemer
National Criminal Justice Reference Service

Note from the Publisher: This report was augmented by a subject index compiled by the publisher.

INTRODUCTION

The Law Enforcement Assistance Administration (LEAA) Task Force on Women was established by LEAA Administrator Richard W. Velde in May 1975. The task force's mission was to develop recommendations for programs to meet the special needs of women within the criminal justice system—female criminal justice professionals, offenders, and victims. As stated in *The Report of the LEAA Task Force on Women* (hereafter referred to as the 1975 report) women working in the criminal justice system at that time were excluded from many jobs, denied opportunities for advancement, and paid less for performing the same work as their male counterparts. FBI statistics showed that crimes—primarily property crimes—committed by women were increasing exponentially. Female arrest rates were rising much faster than male arrest rates. Serious female juvenile crime had quadrupled since 1960. In addition, the criminal justice system was largely unresponsive to the needs of female offenders and female victims of crime. The task force was charged with identifying areas that needed change, starting the processes of change, and recommending methods for change to be pursued by federal and state criminal justice systems.

The task force was charged with the following responsibilities:

(1) Preparing for the LEAA Administrator a policy statement on women's issues addressing the following areas:

- Women as recipients in the LEAA delivery system.
- The concerns and interests of women as part of the states' comprehensive planning process.
- Women in the criminal justice system as offenders, victims, volunteers, and personnel.

(2) Developing program recommendations supporting the policy statement prepared by the task force.

(3) Determining the feasibility of establishing an ongoing effort within LEAA for coordinating women's programs and policies.

The 1975 report discussed the lack of attention given to gender-specific services for women and girls in federal and state criminal justice systems as well as the obstacles facing women employed by law enforcement and other criminal justice agencies, including women employed by LEAA itself [the agency that evolved into today's Office of Justice Programs (OJP)]. In the process of writing the 1975 report, the LEAA Task Force found that the lack of attention given to programs for women and girls was due primarily to inadequate awareness of their special needs and to the priority given to male-specific programs.

Members of the LEAA Task Force were surprised not only that there was so little attention given to women and girls, but also that there was such a lack of information pertaining to them. Prior to 1975, little consideration had been given to collecting or analyzing information on women and girls in the criminal and juvenile justice systems. As a result, many recommendations in the 1975 report required the initial steps of collecting new data and analyzing existing data.

As part of its efforts to carry out the 1975 LEAA Task Force's vision, the OJP Coordination Group on Women, established in November 1994 by Assistant Attorney General Laurie Robinson, has updated the 1975 report. This revised and expanded report provides relevant and important information as well as recommendations for policies, practices, and programs for women and girls in federal and state criminal justice systems and identifies key areas for further study.[*]

The objective of the OJP Coordination Group on Women is to sharpen the focus on women and girls as offenders and victims and the needs of *all* females within the criminal justice and juvenile justice systems. Through improved intra-agency and interagency information exchange, coordinated planning, and collaboration on projects, this objective can be accomplished.

---

[*] Although this report was originally intended to be a 20-year update of *The Report of the LEAA Task Force on Women,* wherever possible, the most up-to-date information is provided.

EXECUTIVE SUMMARY

This monograph is an update of *The Report of the LEAA* [Law Enforcement Assistance Administration] *Task Force on Women,* published in October 1975 (hereafter referred to as the 1975 report).[1] It evaluates the 1975 recommendations made on issues that the criminal justice field should examine to ensure that women and girls are treated fairly in the criminal justice system.

Female offenders, female crime victims, and female criminal justice professionals remain substantially neglected populations in the criminal and juvenile justice systems.[2] Despite the gains made by women since 1975, current evidence shows that:

- ❑ Although the nature and composition of female offenders have changed, the special needs of the burgeoning adult and juvenile offender populations often remain overlooked.
- ❑ Although assistance to crime victims has improved, the need remains for a firm commitment from the criminal justice and juvenile justice systems to change the way these systems respond to women and girls who have been, or potentially could be, victims of crime.

---

[1] Law Enforcement Assistance Administration. October 1975. *The Report of the LEAA Task Force on Women.* Washington, DC: U.S. Department of Justice.

[2] Several resources are available on this topic:
Acoca, L. and J. Austin. 1996. *The Crisis: Women in Prison, Draft Report.* San Francisco, CA: National Council on Crime and Delinquency.
House, C.H. 1993. "The changing role of women in law enforcement." *The Police Chief* 60(10):139–144
Schulz, D. 1994. "California dreaming: Leading the way to gender-free police management." *The Americas,* 7(3) June–July:1, 8–10.

- Although opportunities for female criminal justice professionals have improved, gender bias and inequality still exist within the criminal justice field and women's progress through the ranks continues to be slow.

ADULT FEMALE OFFENDERS

Evidence shows that greater emphasis should be placed on the concerns of and programs for adult female offenders. In 1995, more women were arrested, convicted, and sent to prison than ever before; female offenders made up 6.3 percent of the state and federal prison populations, an increase from 3.8 in 1975. The nature of the crimes women are convicted for today has also changed. In 1975, women were most likely to be incarcerated for crimes such as larceny, forgery, embezzlement, and prostitution. In 1995, an increasing percentage of women were sentenced to prison for drug offenses.

Unfortunately, this increase in the number of female offenders has not been matched by enhanced attention to specialized programs geared particularly for women—such as medical care and counseling for prior victimization from battering or sexual assault, health care, drug treatment, and parenting skills training. This is especially true in light of the criminal justice system's recent adoption of a more punitive philosophy. Thus, programs that address particular women's needs continue to suffer.

JUVENILE FEMALE OFFENDERS

Over the years, many judicial systems have been more interested in detaining and committing female juvenile offenders than in providing community-based services that effectively address their problems. The 1975 report discussed how the criminal justice system failed to provide girls with gender-specific services, such as sexual exploitation and abuse counseling, substance abuse treatment, or parenting skills training. Significant legislative milestones have contributed to the development of the juvenile justice system and its treatment of girls today; however, as with adult corrections, prevention and intervention services are still geared primarily toward males. Despite the lessons learned by criminal justice professionals about this population, girls are still seriously neglected by the juvenile justice system.

WOMEN AND GIRLS AS VICTIMS OF CRIME

In 1994, women were the victims of about 5 million violent crimes.[3] Women were victimized about five times more often than men by persons with whom they had intimate relationships—spouses, former spouses, or boyfriends/girlfriends.[4]

Many factors inhibit women from reporting these crimes either to police or to government interviewers. The private nature of the event, the perceived stigma, and the belief that no purpose can be served by reporting the crime prevent an unknown portion of victims from talking about the event. The 1975 report discussed how the criminal justice system was unresponsive to the needs of female victims of crime. If a woman was assaulted, particularly by an intimate or family member, criminal justice personnel tended to regard the victim as being to blame for her injury and treated her accordingly. Since 1975, public attention has been increasingly devoted to violence against women and the attendant criminal justice response.

Women and girls have benefited from this recent explosion of interest in assisting victims of crime in this country. Changes such as the criminalization of domestic violence and the establishment of sexual assault treatment centers demonstrate the recognition of the serious nature of such crimes. The 1994 Crime Act included the Violence Against Women Act, which provided additional rights to victims of stalking, domestic violence, and sexual assault. Current data on violence against women and girls illustrate the need for a continuing, coordinated, and integrated approach to address these problems.

FEMALE CRIMINAL JUSTICE PROFESSIONALS

Women have always had to struggle for acceptance as professionals in the criminal justice field. Gender inequity is deeply rooted in the workplace and is based on societal expectations and attitudes. Women have had to face many drawbacks and obstacles in male-dominated areas such as law enforcement, corrections, and the courts. Nonetheless, many women have maintained an interest in the criminal justice field and have developed successful careers.

---

[3] Craven, Diane. 1997. *Sex Differences in Violent Victimizations, 1994.* Bureau of Justice Statistics Special Report. Washington, DC: U.S. Department of Justice.
[4] Ibid.

Historically, only nursing, teaching, and clerical positions were open to women in institutions with male inmates. A small number of women worked as correctional officers in these institutions in the early 1970s, but their assignments were limited to peripheral tasks. Thus, the integration of women into previously all-male custodial staffs in men's prisons has been a considerable social change.

Similarly, in law enforcement, women were traditionally limited to working in juvenile facilities, handling crimes involving female offenders, and performing clerical tasks. In the past, women were not considered as capable as men in law enforcement. Female lawyers and judges were often assigned to represent or decide cases in areas traditionally considered the purview of women—family and civil matters.

ACTIONS FOR POLICYMAKERS TO CONSIDER

The following is a list of recommendations for actions that policymakers should consider to meet the needs of women in federal, state, and local criminal justice systems today:

- ❑ Continue gender-specific programming for adult and juvenile female offenders.
- ❑ Encourage the expansion of intermediate sanctions and community programs that address the criminogenic behaviors of female offenders.
- ❑ Allocate more resources to provide the necessary program opportunities to return female offenders to the community.
- ❑ Create more alternatives to abusive home situations.
- ❑ Develop and implement continuum-of-care programs for girls in communities nationwide.
- ❑ Develop new correctional agency policies using examples of promising practices to enhance victim services.
- ❑ Expand juvenile victimization prevention programs.
- ❑ Develop techniques to collect data on crimes committed against victims under the age of 12.
- ❑ Develop strategies to enhance job opportunities for women.
- ❑ Implement policies promoting flexibility in criminal justice agencies to enable all employees to balance careers and family life.
- ❑ Provide staff development and training programs for criminal justice personnel that include assertiveness training, strategic

planning, and workplace diversity initiatives. Emphasize the importance of eliminating sexual harassment in the workplace.

Chapter 1

ADULT FEMALE OFFENDERS

INTRODUCTION

The Report of the LEAA [Law Enforcement Assistance Administration] *Task Force on Women* (hereafter referred to as the 1975 report) characterized women in prison as the "forgotten offenders" because of their small number relative to the male population and because they called so little attention to themselves (women's institutions witnessed few, if any, riots).[1] The 1975 report described the general lack of attention given to adult female offenders' needs within the U.S. criminal justice system and concluded that this neglect stemmed primarily from a lack of awareness of the special needs of female offenders and from the priority given to male-specific programs.

In 1997, more women were arrested, convicted, and sent to prison than ever before.[*] Female offenders made up 6.4 percent of the state and federal prison populations, an increase from 3.8 in 1975. The nature of the crimes women are convicted of has also changed. In 1975, women were most likely to be incarcerated for crimes such as larceny, forgery, embezzlement, and prostitution. Two decades later, the percentage of women sentenced to prison for drug offenses had increased so that in 1995, women were primarily incarcerated for drug-related offenses and larceny. Exhibits 1-1 and 1-2 show the changes in adult female offenders' profiles from 1975 to 1995.

---

[1] Law Enforcement Assistance Administration. October 1975. *The Report of the LEAA Task Force on Women.* Washington, DC: U.S. Department of Justice.

[*] The statistical information presented in this report is the most up-to-date that was available at the time the report was written.

> **Exhibit 1–1**
> **Adult Female Offender Profile in 1975**
>
> - Women represented 13 percent of all arrests in the nation.
> - Women were primarily incarcerated for larceny, forgery, embezzlement, and prostitution.
> - Women constituted 10 percent of all arrests for violent crime.
> - Women represented 5 percent of offenders serving federal prison sentences and 4 percent of offenders serving state prison sentences.[2]
> - Seventy-three percent of incarcerated women had one or more dependent children.

Note: The information presented in this exhibit represents a compilation of the best data available for this time period.

> **Exhibit 1–2**
> **Adult Female Offender Profile in 1995**
>
> - Women represented 19 percent of all arrests in the nation.
> - Women were primarily incarcerated for drug-related offenses and larceny.
> - Women constituted 14 percent of all arrests for violent crime.
> - Women represented 7 percent of offenders serving federal prison sentences and 6 percent of offenders serving state prison sentences.
> - Sixty-one percent of incarcerated women in the federal system and 67 percent in the state systems had one or more children under age 18.[3]

Note: The information presented in this exhibit represents a compilation of the best data available for this time period.

Although the profile of adult female offenders has changed since 1975, the gender-specific needs of female offenders have not changed nor, for the most part, has the criminal justice system's relative inattention to the needs of this population.

Adult female offenders have needs that differ from those of men, stemming in part from female offenders' disproportionate victimization from sexual or physical abuse and their responsibility for children. Female offenders are also more likely to be addicted to drugs and to have mental illnesses. Many states and jail jurisdictions, particularly those with small

---

[2] Law Enforcement Assistance Administration. 1977. *Prisoners in State and Federal Institutions on December 31, 1975*, p. 36. Washington, DC: U.S. Department of Justice.

[3] Harlow, Caroline. 1994. *Comparing Federal and State Prison Inmates, 1991*, p. 17. Bureau of Justice Statistics Report. Washington, DC: U.S. Department of Justice.

female offender populations, have few special provisions, either in management or programming, for meeting the needs of women.[4]

Although some improvements have been made since 1975, largely because of litigation and increased attention to women's issues overall, a great deal needs to be done to ensure that women are treated fairly as they move through every phase of the criminal justice system.

Female offenders require special attention in the following areas:

- Arrests, convictions, and incarceration.
- Gender bias and disparity in sentencing.
- Classification and screening.
- Gender-specific program needs.

ARRESTS, CONVICTIONS, AND INCARCERATION

Data published by the Bureau of Justice Statistics (BJS) show an overall increase in the percentage of female arrestees between 1975 and 1995 (see exhibits 1–3 and 1–4). In 1995, women made up 14.7 percent of all felony defendants convicted in U.S. District Courts, and 58.2 percent of these women were sentenced to federal prisons.[5] In 1994, 15 percent of the felony defendants who appeared in state courts in the nation's 75 largest counties were women.[6] Fifteen percent of all persons convicted in state courts in 1994 were women.[7]

The number of women in prisons and jails is growing at a faster rate than the number of men. Between 1985 and 1995, the number of incarcerated men doubled, increasing from 691,800 to 1,437,600. However, during that same period the number of incarcerated women tripled, rising from 40,500 to 113,100.

---

[4] Morash, Merry, Timothy S. Bynum, and Barbara A. Koons. 1998. *Women Offenders: Programming Needs and Promising Approaches.* National Institute of Justice Research in Brief. Washington, DC: U.S. Department of Justice.

[5] Bureau of Justice Statistics. 1998. *Compendium of Federal Justice Statistics 1995.* Washington, DC: U.S. Department of Justice.

[6] Reaves, Brian A. 1998. *Felony Defendants in Large Urban Counties, 1994.* Washington, DC: U.S. Department of Justice.

[7] Langan, Patrick A. and Jodi M. Brown. 1997. *Felony Sentences in State Courts, 1994.* Bureau of Justice Statistics Special Report. Washington, DC: U.S. Department of Justice.

Exhibit 1–3: Percentage Distribution of Female Arrests by Offense—1975 (based on population of 179 million)	
Murder and nonnegligent manslaughter	15.6
Forcible rape	1.0
Robbery	7.0
Aggravated assault	13.1
Burglary	5.4
Larceny-theft	31.2
Motor vehicle theft	7.0
Arson	11.3
Forgery and counterfeiting	28.9
Fraud	34.2
Embezzlement	31.1
Stolen property	10.7
Vandalism	8.0
Weapons; carrying, possessing, etc.	8.0
Prostitution and commercialized vice	74.3
Sex offenses	7.7
Drug abuse violations	13.8
Gambling	8.8
Offenses against family and children	11.7
DUI	8.1
Liquor law violations	14.3
Disorderly conduct	17.6
Vagrancy	10.5
Curfew and loitering law violations	20.3
Runaways	56.9

Source: Bureau of Justice Statistics, *Sourcebook of Criminal Justice Statistics, 1977*, p. 486.

At midyear 1997, women accounted for 6.4 percent of all prisoners nationwide, up from 4.1 percent in 1980 and 5.7 percent in 1990.[8] According to BJS, women entered the correctional system in record-breaking numbers in 1995. By the end of that year, an estimated 828,100 women were under correctional supervision (in prison or jail or on probation or parole), which

---

[8] Morash, Merry, Timothy S. Bynum, and Barbara A. Koons. 1998. *Women Offenders: Programming Needs and Promising Approaches*.

amounts to 1 out of every 122 women in the U.S. adult population.[9] By 1995, 63,998 women were incarcerated in prison and 52,136 in local jails.[10]

Exhibit 1–4: Percentage Distribution of Female Arrests by Offense—1995 (based on population of 196 million)

Offense	%
Murder and nonnegligent manslaughter	9.5
Forcible rape	1.2
Robbery	9.3
Aggravated assault	17.7
Burglary	11.1
Larceny-theft	33.3
Motor vehicle theft	13.1
Arson	15.7
Forgery and counterfeiting	35.9
Fraud	41.0
Embezzlement	43.6
Stolen property	14.2
Vandalism	13.6
Weapons; carrying, possessing, etc.	7.9
Prostitution and commercialized vice	61.1
Sex offenses	8.0
Drug abuse violations	16.7
Gambling	15.2
Offenses against family and children	20.2
DUI	14.6
Liquor law violations	18.9
Disorderly conduct	21.7
Vagrancy	19.4
Curfew and loitering law violations	29.6
Runaways	57.4

Source: Bureau of Justice Statistics, *Sourcebook of Criminal Justice Statistics*, 1996, p. 380.

At that time, Oklahoma and Texas had the highest female incarceration rates in the nation, while Vermont and Maine had the lowest. In 1975, the

---

[9] Bureau of Justice Assistance. 1997. *Correctional Population in the United States, 1995*. Washington, DC: U.S. Department of Justice.

[10] Gilliard, Darrell K. and Allen J. Beck. 1996. *Prisons and Jail Inmates, 1995*. Bureau of Justice Statistics Bulletin. Washington, DC: U.S. Department of Justice.

proportion of women in federal prisons was 4.6 percent, or about 1,100 inmates; by 1995, the proportion was 7.4 percent, or 7,400 women.

GENDER BIAS AND DISPARITY IN SENTENCING

Gender-based sentencing disparities have been investigated and documented for some 10 years. Lynn Hecht Schafran (National Organization for Women Legal Defense Fund) and Norma Wilker (Senior Research Fellow at the Institute for the Study of Social Change) have noted that the greatest accomplishment of gender bias task forces has been "creating a climate within a court system in which the nature and consequences of judicial gender bias are both acknowledged to exist and understood to be unacceptable."[11] Recognizing the importance of this issue, the Federal Judicial Center published *Studying the Role of Gender in the Federal Courts: A Research Guide* for the study of gender bias in federal courts.[12]

Courts have struck down gender-based disparities in sentencing on equal protection grounds. However, judges continue to accept disparities justified by physiological differences.[13] State-initiated studies are beginning to reveal the extent of bias in sentencing. For example, the Maryland Special Joint Committee on Gender Bias in the Courts asked judges and attorneys if the gender of the parties had affected the litigation processes or outcomes of particular cases.[14] Fifty-two percent of the attorneys and 78 percent of the judges who responded reported that they were aware of such cases. In response to questions regarding credibility problems in the courtroom, female attorneys reported problems with the acceptance of women's testimony in child support, alimony, acquaintance rape, domestic violence, and sexual abuse cases, while male attorneys reported similar problems with women's testimony in personal injury cases. When judges were asked about the severity or leniency of sentencing based on gender, 41 percent reported that women were sentenced *less* severely than men. The committee noted that the most frequently cited reasons for treating women differently were

---

[11] Wikler, N.J. 1990. "Gender and justice: Navigating curves on the road to equality." *Trial* 26(2):36–37.

[12] Gilbert et al. 1995. *Studying the Role of Gender in the Federal Courts: A Research Guide.* Washington, DC: Federal Judicial Center.

[13] Bershad, Lawrence. 1985. "Discriminatory treatment of the female offender in the criminal justice system." *Boston College Law Review* 26(2):289–438.

[14] Maryland Special Joint Committee on Gender Bias in the Courts. 1989. "Gender Bias in the Courts." Honorable Hilary D. Caplan, Chair. Rockville, MD: National Criminal Justice Reference Service.

pregnancy and child care responsibilities. It added, however, that if child care were such a compelling reason for treating women leniently, one would expect to see a greater degree of difference between the percentages of men and women sentenced within the sentencing guidelines.

Myrna S. Raeder reported in the *Pepperdine Law Review* that current male-based sentencing guidelines are inconsistent with developing rational sentencing policies for nonviolent female offenders who constitute the majority of incarcerated women.[15] Raeder also notes that current sentencing guidelines have resulted in higher rates of imprisonment for economic crimes, an area that includes a disproportionate number of women. The article states, "Not only do guidelines help ensure that more women are being incarcerated, but that women now spend more time in prison."[16] Further, although average sentences for property crimes have decreased since 1986, the average percentage of sentence served to *first* release has increased. Raeder advocates the abolition of mandatory minimums at the federal level, suggesting that they frustrate any attempt to create a rational sentencing policy for females, particularly given their gendered roles in criminality.[17]

Literature reveals considerable disagreement regarding the role of gender in sentencing disparity. In their article, "Sex effects and sentencing," Kathleen Daly and Rebecca L. Bordt suggest that sentencing research should move beyond analyses of disparity and the limits that an equal treatment model imposes on empirical studies of justice. They also suggest that gender gaps may be explained largely by the characteristics and severity of men's and women's current and previous lawbreaking activities.[18] Research on disparities and gender bias in sentencing continues.[19]

---

[15] Raeder, Myrna S. "The forgotten offender: The effect of the Sentencing Guidelines and Mandatory Minimums on women and their children." Sent to the Task Group as an update to Raeder, Myrna S. 1993. "Gender and sentencing: Single moms, battered women and other sex-based anomalies in the gender-free world of the Sentencing Guidelines." *Pepperdine Law Review* 20(3):905–991.

[16] Ibid.

[17] Ibid.

[18] Daly, Kathleen and Rebecca L. Bordt. 1995. "Sex effects and sentencing: An analysis of the statistical literature." *Justice Quarterly* 12(1):141–175.

[19] As noted in the 1994 *U.S. Sentencing Commission Annual Report*, results are pending on the following projects: Just Punishment Research Project, Selective Incapacitation Project, and Study of Changing Composition of Offenses and Offenders Projects.

CLASSIFICATION AND SCREENING

Classification and screening are important tools for managing offenders and are effective for meeting offender housing and program needs. The 1991 National Institute of Corrections (NIC) review of classification practices found that states use identical classification systems for men and women. Recognizing that a strict gender-based approach to classification may ultimately lead to disparities and legal problems, NIC recommended an approach that supports institution-specific objectives. NIC suggested that the population used in designing the classification instrument should include women and men in sufficient numbers and proportion to ensure that any new system would be relevant to both genders. The resulting report, *Classification of Women Offenders in State Correctional Facilities: A Handbook for Practitioners,* serves as a reference for policymakers and a resource for practitioners who work with female offenders.[20]

The Gathering Information, Assessing What Works, Interpreting the Facts, Networking with Key Stakeholders, and Stimulating Change (GAINS) Center's study, "Specific Needs of Women in Correctional Facilities," found that women are typically underserved in all types of incarceration programs.[21] Furthermore, the study reported that services for female inmates in such areas as mental health or substance abuse are based on models designed for males. For the criminal justice system to be more responsive to women's needs, programs should be tailored to meet their special requirements, as indicated by their classification information.

Screening is an essential aspect of classification, and mental health is an area in which screening is required. In a study of innovative and promising programs for women, sponsored by the National Institute of Justice (NIJ), Merry Morash found a clear connection between the size of the inmate population and the frequency of mental health screening.[22] In her study, the 12 states with more than 1,000 incarcerated women reportedly screened all of the female inmates. States with 500 to 999 incarcerated women reportedly screened 91 percent of the female inmates, states with 100 to 499 reportedly

---

[20] Burke, Peggy and Linda Adams. 1991. *Classification of Women Offenders in State Correctional Facilities: A Handbook for Practitioners.* Washington, DC: National Institute of Corrections.

[21] Gathering Information, Assessing What Works, Interpreting the Facts, Networking with Key Stakeholders, and Stimulating Change (GAINS) Center. February 1996. "Specific Needs of Women in Correctional Facilities." Presented in Washington, DC.

[22] Morash, Merry. 1996. "Findings from the National Study of Innovative and Promising Programs for Women Offenders." National Institute of Justice Research Project. Washington, DC: U.S. Department of Justice.

screened 88 percent, and states with 100 to 499 reportedly screened 62 percent. Prior abuse, parental responsibility, and vocational choice were the areas in which women committed to state correctional institutions received the least amount of screening. Screening for medical status and mental health also requires further attention, particularly because classification and screening should be used to channel women into the least restrictive housing.

GENDER-SPECIFIC PROGRAM NEEDS

The rapid increase in the number of female offenders has not been matched by an increase in specialized programs for them. Prison and jail administrators interviewed for Morash's 1996 study highlighted the lack of programs, lack of space, large populations, and limited resources as key management problems in operations of correctional facilities for men and women.[23]

According to Morash, programs that are designed to meet the specific needs of women should have components that address a woman's prior victimization from battering and abusive relationships; child, sexual, and other abuse; and sexual assault. However, Morash noted that exemplary programs for female offenders are threatened by a lack of funding and by the criminal justice system's adaption of a more punitive philosophy.[24]

Programs that should take into account the special needs of women include the following:

- Substance abuse treatment.
- Health-care services.
- Academic and vocational education.
- Parenting skills.
- Community corrections and intermediate sanctions.

SUBSTANCE ABUSE TREATMENT

The increased presence of women in the criminal justice system—from an increased percentage of female arrestees to an increase in the percentage of women imprisoned—has been accompanied by a growing recognition that

---

[23] Ibid.
[24] Ibid.

a substantial proportion of these women enter the system because of their involvement with drugs. In 1975, women were more likely to be arrested for larceny, forgery, embezzlement, and prostitution. During the past decade, both drug offenses by women and the proportion of female offenders who are substance abusers have increased dramatically. This population continues to escalate despite an increase in deterrents such as tougher sentencing laws and a crackdown on drug offenders.

According to data from NIJ's Arrestee Drug Abuse Monitoring program (formally known as the Drug Use Forecasting program), 67 percent of females arrested in 1994 tested positive for drugs.[25] Female arrestees are much more likely to abuse cocaine and opiates, while male arrestees are more likely to test positive for marijuana use. Lifetime prevalence rates of alcohol abuse/dependance disorders also reveal that female arrestees are more likely than male arrestees to be diagnosed with substance abuse disorders—70.2 percent of female arrestees compared with 32.4 percent of male arrestees.[26]

Women in state prisons were more likely than their male counterparts to be drug involved (see exhibit 1–5). Roughly 54 percent of female prisoners in 1991 had used drugs in the month before their offense, compared with 50 percent of the male prisoners.[27] Female inmates were also more likely than male inmates to have used drugs regularly, to report having used a needle to inject illegal drugs, and to have been under the influence of drugs at the time of the offenses. Overall, about half the women reported that they had never participated in a drug treatment or drug education program. The BJS report, *Women in Prison,* found that in 1991 about one in four incarcerated women reported committing their offense to get money to buy drugs. However, drug users were less likely than nonusers to be serving a sentence for a violent offense.

Similarly, among convicted jail inmates in 1996, drug use was more prevalent for women than for men (see exhibit 1–6).[28] According to BJS statistics, an estimated 60 percent of convicted female jail inmates used drugs in the month before their offense compared to 54 percent of convicted males. Women in jail were also more likely to report prior regular drug use or being under the influence of drugs at the time of their offense.

---

[25] National Institute of Justice. 1995. *Drug Use Forecasting: 1994 Annual Report on Adult and Juvenile Arrestees.* Washington, DC: U.S. Department of Justice.

[26] Levin, Bruce Lubosky, Andrea K. Blanch, and Ann Jennings. 1998. *Women's Mental Health Services: A Public Health Perspective.* Thousand Oaks, CA: Sage Publications.

[27] Ibid.

[28] Bureau of Justice Statistics. 1996. *Survey of Inmates in Local Jails.* Unpublished data.

Exhibit 1–5
Drug-Use History of State Prison Inmates in 1991

Drug-Use Information	Percentage of Inmates Female	Male
Ever used	79.5	79.4
Used regularly for at least one month	65.3	62.0
Used in the month before current offense	53.9	49.6
Used daily in the month before current offense	41.4	35.7
Under the influence at the time of the current offense	36.3	30.6
Committed offense to get money to buy drugs	23.9	16.5

Source: Snell, Tracy L. 1994. *Women in Prison*, p. 7, Bureau of Justice Statistics Special Report.

Exhibit 1–6
Prior Drug Use of Convicted Jail Inmates by Gender in 1996

Drug-Use Information	Percentage of Inmates Female	Male
Ever used	85.6	84.3
Used regularly for at least one month	73.2	66.0
Used in the month before current offense	60.4	54.4
Used daily in the month before current offense	-------	------
Under the influence at the time of the current offense	43.6	34.7
Committed offense to get money to buy drugs	-------	------

Source: *Survey of Inmates in Local Jails*. 1996. Bureau of Justice Statistics. Unpublished data.

A large percentage of the adult female offender population continues to be drug-use violators. In 1975, about 30 percent of the women in federal facilities were drug offenders;[29] in 1996 the figure was 68 percent.[30] Today, however, women who are convicted of drug offenses are often only couriers or "front" people. Despite not having a major role in such drug transactions, women are sometimes sent to prison for longer periods of time than men involved in more extensive drug distribution. In many cases, women commit their crimes to pay for their own drug addiction.

---

[29] Bureau of Justice Statistics. 1978. *Sourcebook of Criminal Justice Statistics, 1977*, p. 668. Washington, DC: U.S. Department of Justice.
[30] Bureau of Justice Statistics. 1997. *Sourcebook of Criminal Justice Statistics, 1996*, p. 533. Washington, DC: U.S. Department of Justice.

The unique needs of women and increased drug abuse and drug-related arrests of female offenders have changed the emphasis of correctional programming for this population. Programs and services needed for female offenders range from medical and mental health to life skills. There is a particular need for drug education and drug treatment programs.

HEALTH-CARE SERVICES

Specific health-care services are required not only for pregnant inmates but for female offenders in general, since most inmates have rarely received medical or dental examinations or prenatal care. Proper screening and infection control programs are vital aspects of correctional health care prior to incarceration. Behavior that often leads to incarceration—intravenous drug use, violence, and prostitution, for example—places inmates at high risk for HIV, tuberculosis (TB), and hepatitis.[31] A Northwestern University study suggested substantial psychiatric morbidity among the 1,272 female detainees awaiting trial between 1991 and 1993 at the Cook County (Illinois) Jail. The most common disorders were drug abuse or dependence, alcohol abuse or dependence, and posttraumatic stress disorder.[32] The need to include substance abuse education and treatment programs for women offenders in an overall health-care program is reinforced when it is noted that female drug users are much more likely to have committed robbery, burglary, larceny, and fraud than females who do not use drugs.[33]

The risk factor is tragic when drugs, needles, and sex are combined. In 1992, 73 women died in state prisons, 29 of whom had AIDS.[34] Women in the prison and jail systems are significantly more likely to be HIV-positive than men. As of 1995, 4 percent of the women in state prisons were HIV-positive compared with 2.3 percent of the men.[35] There is also a connection between TB bacteria and HIV; individuals infected with both diseases

---

[31] Campbell, Mark K. 1993. "Infection Control: Managing Exposure to Communicable Diseases." The State of Corrections, 1992. Lanham, MD: American Correctional Association.

[32] Teplin, Linda, A. Teplin, Karen M. Abram, and Gary M. McClellan. Cited in *Arch Gen Psychiatry* 53:505–512.

[33] Corrothers, Helen G. 1998. "Prevention and Intervention: Stemming the Flow—Complex Challenges and Collaborative Solutions: Programming for Adult and Juvenile Offenders." Lanham, MD: American Correctional Association.

[34] Snell, Tracy L. 1993. *Correctional Populations in the United States, 1992*, p. 83. Washington, DC: U.S. Department of Justice.

[35] Maruschak, Laura. 1997. *HIV in Prisons and Jails,* p. 6. Washington, DC: U.S. Department of Justice.

present an extraordinary risk of spreading TB to other inmates and facility staff. Every correctional facility should have a program in place to handle a TB outbreak.[36]

ACADEMIC AND VOCATIONAL EDUCATION

Although correctional education was established with the first prison in 1798, education has not always been seen as a necessary expense in the allocation of resources. At the state level, each legislative body decides whether a general educational development program is mandatory for its institutions. The Correctional Education Association (CEA), an affiliate of the American Correctional Association (ACA), is the only professional organization for educators working in the criminal justice system. CEA provides standards for state and federal adult correctional educators, one of which is mandatory: women's equity. CEA standards specify that women should not be denied equal access to comparable programs and services solely because they are a small proportion of the offender population.[37] On average, a higher percentage of females than males participate in education programs in the federal system—in fact, in 1996, 47 percent of female inmates, compared with 29 percent of male inmates, participated in one or more educational programs.[38]

The Federal Bureau of Prisons (BOP) has mandated a general educational development program for its facilities. Inmates who enter the prison system without a high school diploma or general equivalency diploma (GED) are required to attend literacy classes for 120 days or until they achieve a GED. A recent BOP study concluded that participation in prison educational programs reduces the likelihood of recidivism, irrespective of postrelease employment.

Vocational training programs are also important. A BJS survey conducted in 1991 found that female inmates were significantly less likely than male inmates to be employed at the time of arrest (47 percent employed versus 68 percent employed, respectively).[39] There is an urgent need for programs to develop job skills and good work habits among female inmates

---

[36] Eales, H. Parker. 1993. "TB, HIV and MDR–TB–A Tragic Combination." *The State of Corrections, 1992.* Lanham, MD: American Correctional Association.
[37] Correctional Education Association. 1988. "Standards for Adult and Juvenile Correctional Educational Programs." College Park, MD.
[38] Federal Bureau of Prisons. 1996. *Program Report.* Washington, DC: U.S. Department of Justice.
[39] Snell, Tracy L. *Women in Prison.*

because, upon release, these women most often provide support for their families.[40]

ACA recognizes that the availability of a comprehensive academic and vocational education for offenders is vital to their successful reintegration into the community. The promulgation of nationally recognized standards for correctional institutions, agencies, and programs seeking accreditation should provide eligible offenders with (1) a program to improve communication skills, (2) general education, (3) basic academic skills, (4) GED preparation, (5) vocational training, (6) postsecondary education, and (7) other education programs as dictated by the needs of the population. Further, standards should require that academic and vocational programs be recognized, certified, or licensed by the state department of education or other agencies having jurisdiction. The Standards Committee of ACA is presently developing performance-based standards that will measure the degree to which the effect intended by a standard is achieved.[41]

PARENTING SKILLS

The majority of female inmates are mothers, and as such have many special program needs. A 1991 BJS survey reported that about 78 percent of female inmates have children, most of whom have children under 18 years old.[42] The proportion of incarcerated women who are mothers has remained constant since 1975. With each mother having an average of 2.5 children, there are now close to a quarter of a million children whose mothers are incarcerated.

One out of every four adult women in prison is pregnant at the time of incarceration or has given birth at some point during the previous year.[43] John D. Wooldredge and Kimberly Masters surveyed wardens of state prisons in 1991 and found that less than 50 percent had written policies specifically relating to medical care for pregnant inmates and only 48 percent offered prenatal services. Of the facilities in this second category, 21 percent offered prenatal counseling, 15 percent offered counseling to help mothers

---

[40] Corrothers, Helen G. 1998. "Prevention and Intervention: Stemming the Flow—Complex Challenges and Collaborative Solutions: Programming for Adult and Juvenile Offenders."
[41] Verdeyen, Robert J. 1996. American Correctional Association interview with Helen G. Corrothers.
[42] Snell, Tracy L. *Women in Prison*, pp. 6, 7.
[43] Wooldredge, John D. and Kimberly Masters. 1993. "Confronting problems faced by pregnant inmates in State prisons." *Crime and Delinquency* 39(2):195–203.

find suitable placement for the infant after birth, and 15 percent had policies for lighter or no work during pregnancy.

In 1991, about 67 percent of women in state prisons (see exhibit 1–7) and 61 percent in federal prisons had children younger than age 18.[44] According to *Women in Prison*, only 25 percent of female state prisoners in 1991 indicated that they had any children living with the father; children of incarcerated women were most often living with grandparents. About 90 percent of incarcerated women with children under 18 years of age had some contact with their children—by telephone, mail, or visitation while serving their prison term. An estimated 46 percent of women with minor children said they had telephone conversations with their children at least once a week; 45 percent had mail contact at least once a week; and 9 percent had weekly visits with their children.[45]

Exhibit 1–7
Parental Status of State Prison Inmates in 1991

Parental Status	All State Inmates (%)	Male State Inmates (%)	Female State Inmates (%)
No Children	35.3	36.1	21.9
Have Children	64.7	63.9	78.1
Children Under Age 18	56.7	56.1	66.6
Adult Children Only	7.9	7.6	11.5

Source: Harlow, Caroline W. 1994. *Comparing Federal and State Prison Inmates: 1991*, p. 17, Bureau of Justice Statistics.

State policies and procedures determine the extent to which women can maintain contact with their children. Having only one facility in a state for female inmates causes visitation problems not faced by male inmates—the cost of travel to the facility, availability of transportation, and the availability of someone to bring children to visit. In a 1983 article, Linda Abram Koban points out that when men are incarcerated their children most often remain with their mother on the outside. This situation may allow for more

---

[44] Harlow, Caroline W. 1994. *Comparing Federal and State Prison Inmates: 1991*. Bureau of Justice Statistics Report, p. 17. Washington, DC: U.S. Department of Justice.
[45] Snell, Tracy L. *Women in Prison*, p. 5.

visitations, since mothers can bring the children to visit more often. Moreover, men are often incarcerated closer to their homes than women.[46]

Visitation is a very important component of most parenting programs. The National Advisory Commission on Criminal Justice advocates that correctional authorities should encourage visitors rather than merely tolerate them. Correctional authorities should not limit the number of visitors an offender may receive or the length of visits except in accordance with regular institutional standards. In fact, correctional authorities should promote visitation by providing transportation for visitors from terminal points of public transportation, by providing rooms that allow informal communication in a comfortable environment, and by making provisions for family visits in private surroundings conducive to strengthening family ties.[47]

Several successful parenting programs are currently operating in women's correctional facilities. The Girl Scouts Behind Bars program, originated by NIJ in 1992 in a Maryland women's prison, met with success and is being replicated in several states, including Arizona, Delaware, Florida, Kentucky, New Jersey, and Ohio. Under this program, mothers and daughters attend a Girl Scout troop meeting in a prison or jail two Saturdays each month. Mothers spend supervised time working on troop projects with their daughters. Topics range from aerobics to math and science activities to arts and crafts. Issues such as increasing self-esteem, avoiding drug abuse, coping with family crises, and preventing teenage pregnancy are also addressed creatively. The Mothers With Infants Together (MINT) program, allows eligible pregnant offenders to reside in a community-based program for 2 months prior to delivery to prepare for birth and for 3 months after delivery to bond with their baby. MINT was created in 1994 in Fort Worth, Texas, by the Volunteers of America and has served as a model for other correctional systems nationwide. Women are referred to MINT by sentencing judges or federal institutions. The MINT program allows mothers to participate in prenatal and postnatal programs on issues such as childbirth, parenting and family support skills, family literacy, and substance abuse education.[48]

---

[46] Koban, Linda Abram. 1983. "Parents in prison: A comparative analysis of the effects of incarceration on the families of men and women." *Research in Law, Deviance, and Social Control* 5:171–183.

[47] Schafer, N.E. 1991. "Prison visiting policies and practices." *International Journal of Offender Therapy and Comparative Criminology* 35(3):263–275.

[48] Williams, Elizabeth Friar. 1996. "Fostering the Mother-Child Bond in a Correctional Setting." *Corrections Today* 58(6): 80–81.

COMMUNITY CORRECTIONS AND INTERMEDIATE SANCTIONS

There are some innovative alternatives and facilities that address the needs of female offenders today. Community corrections and intermediate sanctions, for example, combine supervision and services to address the needs of female offenders in highly structured, safe environments in which accountability is stressed.

Recognition of the unique needs of women has resulted in considerable concern about gender equality in the development of intermediate sanctions programs. Correctional professionals widely believe that many more female offenders are eligible for intermediate sanctions than are currently placed in these programs. A female boot camp program that provides both treatment and services—including aftercare services—would be ideal.

Boot camps, also referred to as shock incarceration, are modeled after military basic training and emphasize strict discipline and respect for authority. Normally the daily schedule includes military drills and ceremonies, physical training, and demanding work assignments. The programs generally target nonviolent, first-time offenders. The use of a treatment model can be designed to support the often differing emotional needs of women and their need for drug treatment and vocational training.[49]

Home confinement is another intermediate sanction that may be well suited for female offenders. Home confinement allows inmates to reside at home with a strict curfew. Inmates must remain home during specified periods, usually nonwork hours and on weekends.

BOP has created comprehensive sanction centers that are multifaceted, community-based, and expand halfway house services with a range of supervision/accountability programs aimed at reaching a broad spectrum of male and female offenders. These programs are designed to provide the courts with a wide range of sentencing options, particularly for supervising offenders who revert to substance abuse. They are also designed to provide prerelease services to high-need inmates returning to the community. Aftercare and transitional services are especially important for incarcerated women as they return to the community. Community-based treatment and programming are also needed for female offenders who are incarcerated.

Community-based drug treatment involves intensive outpatient counseling and drug testing. Research and experience demonstrate that a

---

[49] Gowdy, Voncile. 1996. "A Critical Look at Boot Camps for Women." In *Juvenile and Adult Boot Camps*. Lanham, MD: American Correctional Association.

critical component of an inmate's transition back into the community is effective substance abuse treatment. When possible, the same treatment providers are used by BOP and the U.S. Probation Service to ensure continuity of care upon completion of the sentence. Although progress has been made since 1975 in the development and implementation of community-based and intermediate sanctions, enhancement and expansion need to continue.

RECOMMENDATIONS FROM THE OJP COORDINATION GROUP ON WOMEN

1. Continue gender-specific programming for adult and juvenile female offenders.
2. Collect more gender-specific data at every point in the criminal justice process to establish an accurate profile of the female offender.
3. Ensure that specialized training is provided to law enforcement personnel, including the development of emergency services, alternatives to arrest, and mental health crisis intervention. Train staff on women's issues, listening skills, and services that are available to women in the community.
4. Encourage the expansion of intermediate sanctions and community programs that address the criminogenic behaviors of female offenders.
5. Develop state department of corrections policy standards for community release specific to female offenders, and develop staff training curriculums to prepare probation and parole officers to manage women's many needs in the community.
6. Emphasize the study and management of older female offenders, since their numbers are expected to increase.
7. Allocate more resources to provide the necessary program opportunities to return female offenders to the community.
8. Offer mental health and substance abuse treatment programs to women in jails and prisons.
9. Assess and provide additional services for women who have histories of physical and sexual abuse.
10. Encourage visitation rights, parenting programs, and other opportunities for mothers and children to be together.

Chapter 2

FEMALE JUVENILE OFFENDERS

INTRODUCTION

Historically, institutionalization has been the juvenile justice system's primary response to at-risk girls. Most female juvenile delinquents committed status offenses (running away and truancy) rather than serious crimes. The juvenile justice system concentrated on detaining and committing these status offenders rather than examining the roots of their problems and providing community-based services that effectively addressed them. Although the number of detained cases involving girls is growing at a slower rate than the number of court referrals involving girls, girls are still more likely than boys to be incarcerated for status and minor offenses such as truancy, running away, drinking, curfew violations, incorrigibility, and petty theft.

Professionals in the juvenile justice field now report that in many instances of offense, young women may be acting out as a means of self-protection in response to life-threatening conditions. The underlying cause of female juvenile delinquency has been reported to be family problems, including sexual and/or physical abuse in the home. It is not surprising, therefore, that most female juvenile offenders report that their first arrest was for running away from home to avoid physical and sexual abuse.[1]

Unfortunately commitment is still a frequently used solution when no alternatives are available within the community to assist young women in

---

[1] Chesney-Lind, Meda and Randall G. Shelden. 1992. *Girls, Delinquency and Juvenile Justice.* Pacific Grove, CA: Brooks/Cole.

crisis situations. Programs designed to address the special needs of female delinquents have been and remain inadequate in most states.[2]

FEMALE JUVENILE OFFENDERS IN 1975

The Report of the LEAA [Law Enforcement Assistance Administration] *Task Force on Women* (hereafter referred to as the 1975 report) found that "despite some alarming statistics, female juvenile offenders received little attention from those charged with improving the criminal justice system."[3] The 1975 report also noted that society's sexual double standard was particularly harsh on female juveniles. For example, it was found that girls were more likely than boys to be committed to an institution if there was any evidence of sexual activity, regardless of the offense for which these females had been initially convicted.

A review of the sentencing practices relative to female juvenile offenders demonstrated that regardless of the girl's offense, it was almost invariably accompanied by behavior that was perceived to be socially unacceptable. The task force also noted the lack of research describing characteristics of female juvenile offenders and identifying effective practices and programs for this neglected population.

A major recommendation in the 1975 report called for a comprehensive approach that would focus attention on female juveniles and identify specific strategies for eliminating the discriminatory treatment girls receive in the system. It was recommended that such an approach include a substantial research component to examine issues such as the causes of crime, effective treatment, and alternatives to incarceration for female juvenile offenders.

Specifically, the 1975 report recommended that the Office of Juvenile Justice and Delinquency Prevention (OJJDP):

1. Develop strategies to increase state planning agency (SPA) support for female juvenile offender programs.
2. Review the juvenile delinquency section of all state plans to ensure compliance with SPA guideline 4100.1D requiring that the needs of all disadvantaged youth be analyzed and considered and that

---

[2] Bergsmann, Ilene R. 1994. "Establishing a foundation: Just the facts." In *1994 National Juvenile Female Offenders Conference: A Time For Change,* pp. 3–14. Lanham, MD: American Correctional Association.

[3] Law Enforcement Assistance Administration. 1975. *The Report of the LEAA Task Force on Women,* p. 9. Washington, DC: U.S. Department of Justice.

assistance be available on an equitable basis from federal funds; that a review of other federal, state, local, and private programs affecting these youth be included; and that all programs be broken down by sex and minority group.
3. Develop and fund research that analyzes the treatment of female juveniles by the courts, referral agencies, and the community, with special emphasis on status offenders.
4. Develop and fund discretionary programs that focus on the needs of the female juvenile offenders from referral to postadjudication stages.[4]

To determine the current status of female juvenile offenders and girls at risk, the Office of Justice Programs' (OJP's) Coordination Group on Women reviewed the changes that had taken place in this population between 1975 and 1998. Differences in the types of crimes committed by girls during this period were also assessed.

1975 DATA ON FEMALE JUVENILE OFFENDERS

The following data on female juvenile offenders were provided in the 1975 report:

- *Female Juvenile Arrest Trends.* Girls entered the system at a higher rate, were more likely to be incarcerated for less serious offenses, and were likely to be kept incarcerated for longer periods of time than boys.[5]
- *Females in Juvenile Court.* The ratio of juvenile males to females referred to court was 3 to 1.[6]
- *Females in Juvenile Detention.* Female juveniles represented 24 percent of persons in public juvenile detention centers and correctional facilities. Truancy, incorrigibility, and sexual delinquency were the primary status offenses for which female juveniles were institutionalized.[7]

---

[4] Ibid., pp. 10, 11.
[5] Law Enforcement Assistance Administration. 1975. *The Report of the LEAA Task Force on Women*, p. 9.
[6] Ibid., p. 9, quoting Health Education and Welfare Juvenile Court Statistics. 1973.
[7] Ibid., p. 9.

CURRENT CHARACTERISTICS OF FEMALE JUVENILE OFFENDERS

Beginning in the 1980s and continuing through to 1998, girls started to enter the justice system at younger ages.

- Data between 1987 and 1991 indicate that there was a 10-percent increase in the numbers of 13- and 14-year-old boys and girls coming into juvenile court.[8]
- From 1993 to 1995, the typical female juvenile offender was 15 or 16 years old; belonged to a minority group; was a high school dropout; lived in a poor, inner-city neighborhood; and was frequently a victim of sexual and/or physical abuse or exploitation.[9]
- In the 1990s, most female juvenile offenders are from single-parent families, have been placed in foster care, lack adequate work and social skills, and are substance abusers.[10]
- Female juveniles represent an estimated 6 percent of gang members.[11]

FEMALE JUVENILE ARREST TRENDS

In 1995, U.S. law enforcement agencies arrested an estimated 702,200 females under the age of 18, which was 264,500 more female juvenile offenders than were arrested in 1981. Between 1981 and 1995, arrests of females grew faster than arrests of males (see exhibit 2–1).[12] In their study of female offenders in the juvenile justice system, Eileen Poe-Yamagata and Jeffrey Butts found the following arrest trends and records:

---

[8] National Center for Juvenile Justice. 1994. *Female Juvenile Offenders, Technical Assistance Resource Materials.* Pittsburgh, PA.

[9] Bergsmann, Ilene R. 1994. "Establishing a foundation: Just the facts." In *1994 National Juvenile Female Offenders Conference: A Time For Change,* pp. 3–14. Lanham, MD: American Correctional Association/Office of Juvenile Justice and Delinquency Prevention.

[10] Ibid.

[11] Chesney-Lind, Meda, Randall G. Shelden, and Karen A. Joe. 1996. "Girls, delinquency, and gang membership." In *Gangs in America,* 2d ed., ed. C. Ronald Huff, pp. 185–204. Thousand Oaks, CA: Sage Publications, Inc.

[12] Poe-Yamagata, Eileen and Jeffrey A. Butts. 1996. *Female Offenders in the Juvenile Justice System.* Pittsburgh, PA: National Center for Juvenile Justice.

Exhibit 2-1

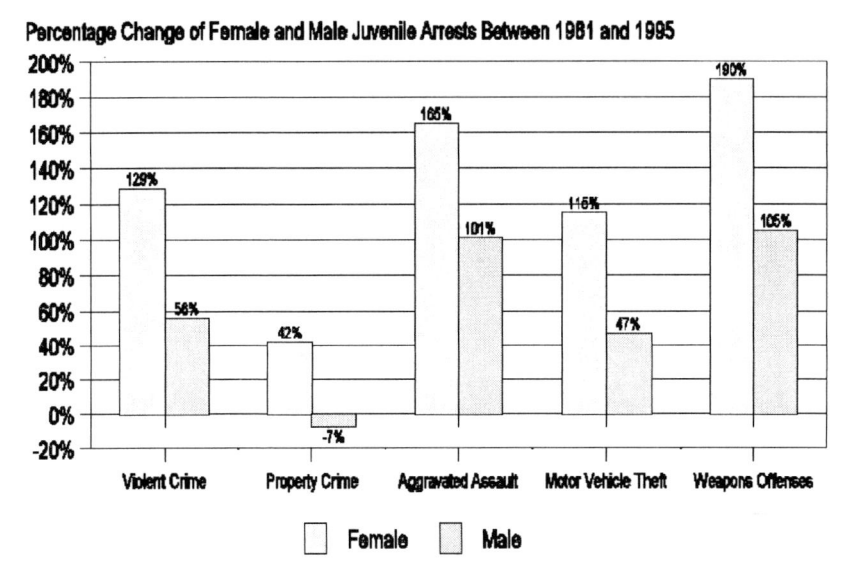

Percentage Change of Female and Male Juvenile Arrests Between 1981 and 1995

Offense	Female	Male
Violent Crime	129%	58%
Property Crime	42%	-7%
Aggravated Assault	165%	101%
Motor Vehicle Theft	115%	47%
Weapons Offenses	190%	105%

Source: Eileen Poe-Yamagata. 1996. *A Statistical Overview of Females in the Juvenile Justice System.* Pittsburgh, PA: National Center for Juvenile Justice.

❑ Between 1986 and 1995, the number of juvenile females arrested increased by 50 percent compared with a 26-percent increase in the arrests of male juveniles.

❑ The female proportion of all juvenile arrests grew from 22 percent to 26 percent between 1986 and 1995.

❑ Females were responsible for 20 percent of the growth in juvenile arrests for Violent Crime Index offenses between 1986 and 1995. The disparate growth in female arrests for Violent Crime Index offenses is the result of the large increase in the number of aggravated assault arrests for female juveniles.

❑ Arrests for Property Crime Index offenses involving female juveniles increased 38 percent between 1986 and 1995, while the number of male arrests for Property Crime Index offenses increased by 1 percent.

❑ Between 1986 and 1995, female juvenile arrests increased more than male juvenile arrests in most non-Index offense categories. For example, arrests for simple assault increased 159 percent for female juveniles and 97 percent for male juveniles. Weapons violations increased 138 percent for female juveniles and 85 percent for male juveniles.[13]

However, while the number of homicides by male juveniles has more than doubled since the mid-1980s, the number of homicides by female juveniles has remained steady over the same period.[14] The typical female juvenile homicide offender is nearly as likely to murder a family member (46 percent) as an acquaintance (41 percent). This behavior is consistent with abuse/victim-oriented offenders.[15]

FEMALES IN JUVENILE COURT

Since the early 1980s, the number of delinquency cases handled by juvenile courts has steadily increased. In 1993, juvenile courts handled an estimated 1,489,700 delinquency cases; girls were involved in 20 percent of these cases, which almost equaled the juvenile female arrest for the same year (24 percent). The juvenile female court cases included person and property offenses.

Between 1985 and 1994, the largest increase in the number of female juvenile offender referrals occurred in the person offense category. During that period, researchers found the following:

- ❏ Female juvenile person offense referrals increased 124 percent; property offense referrals increased 40 percent.

- ❏ More African-American female juveniles were referred for property offenses in 1994 than in 1985. Total female juvenile referrals for property offenses increased 38 percent, whereas the increase for African-American female juveniles was 92 percent.

- ❏ Referrals for person and property offense cases grew faster for girls than for boys.[16]

---

[13] Ibid.
[14] Snyder, Howard N. and Melissa Sickmund. 1995. *Juvenile Offenders and Victims: A Focus on Violence*, p. 56. NCJ 153570. Washington, DC: Office of Juvenile Justice and Delinquency Prevention.
[15] Ibid.
[16] Poe-Yamagata, Eileen. 1996. *A Statistical Overview of Females in the Juvenile Justice System*. Pittsburgh, PA: National Center for Juvenile Justice.

In 1994, juvenile courts in the United States handled an estimated 1.5 million delinquency cases. Female juveniles were involved in 21 percent of these cases and were responsible for 23 percent of all person offense cases. In addition, female juveniles were responsible for 22 percent of property offense cases, 14 percent of drug law violation cases, and 21 percent of public order offense cases (for example, disorderly conduct, weapons offenses, and liquor law violations).[17]

Between 1985 and 1994, the growth in the number of female cases varied depending on how the cases were processed (see exhibit 2–2). The number of females detained (38 percent) grew slower than the number of females referred (54 percent), which led researchers to conclude that there was not enough bed space to detain all referrals. The number of females adjudicated (65 percent) grew less than the number of females petitioned to appear in court (95 percent). And the number of females placed in correctional facilities (47 percent) grew less than the number of females adjudicated, which researchers attribute to insufficient court resources to place the juveniles. Among all offense categories, the increase in the number of females petitioned grew the fastest. The growth in the number of placements out of the home was less than the growth in adjudications among females but not among males.[18]

Exhibit 2–2

Percentage Change of Court Processing Between 1985 and 1994.

Referred	Detained	Petitioned	Adjudicated	Placed	Probation
54%	38%	95%	65%	47%	57%

Source: Eileen Poe-Yamagata. 1996 *A Statistical Overview of Females in the Juvenile Justice System*. Pittsburgh, PA: National Center for Juvenile Justice.

---

[17] Ibid.
[18] Ibid.

Despite the lower likelihood of detention for female juvenile offenders in 1993, the number of juvenile court cases involving detained females increased more in relative terms than the number of detention cases involving males.[19]

FEMALES IN JUVENILE DETENTION

In 1987, 9 percent of all girls in training school were committed for status offenses, compared with only 1.5 percent of boys.[20] The number of girls in detention increased by 2 percent between 1987 and 1991.

In 1993, secure detention was used at some point between referral and disposition in 16 percent of delinquency cases involving females, compared with 22 percent of cases involving males. However, Poe-Yamagata and Butts found that the greatest use of detention for females occurred in drug offense and public order offense cases (both 23 percent). From 1987 to 1993, growth in female property offense cases resulting in detention was more than double the growth in male cases. However, the number of drug offense cases involving detention declined more among females than among males.[21]

By 1993, person offenses accounted for 25 percent of female delinquency cases involving detention, up from 21 percent in 1989. Of the cases that were not dismissed, about one-third of female juvenile offenders were placed on probation. Of the girls who were detained, 20 percent were placed in a special program; only 3 percent of nondetained girls received such placements.[22]

CHANGES SINCE 1975

Significant legislative milestones have contributed to the development of the juvenile justice system and its treatment of girls today. In 1974, just prior to publication of the 1975 report, the Juvenile Justice and Delinquency

---

[19] Ibid.
[20] Schwartz, Ira M., Martha W. Steketee, and Victoria W. Schneider. 1989. *The Incarceration of Girls: Paternalism or Crime Control?* Ann Arbor, MI: Center for the Study of Youth Policy.
[21] Poe-Yamagata, Eileen and Jeffrey A. Butts. *Female Offenders in the Juvenile Justice System.*
[22] Ibid.

Prevention (JJDP) Act[23]—which created OJJDP—was enacted to respond to widespread concerns about juvenile crime. The enactment of the JJDP Act helped to implement a major recommendation of the 1975 report, which called for the deinstitutionalization of status offenders. The 1977 reauthorization of the JJDP Act reaffirmed congressional support for separating juveniles from adults and removing status offenders from secure settings. The deinstitutionalization of status offenders directly affected females in the juvenile justice system because, at that time, most girls who became involved with the juvenile justice system were status offenders. Since that time a number of changes have occurred in both what is known about female juveniles and how the juvenile justice system responds to them. However, in spite of the increased awareness and the changes that have been made, many needs of female juvenile offenders remain unmet. Girls are still seriously neglected in the juvenile justice system.

LEGISLATIVE HISTORY OF THE JUVENILE JUSTICE AND DELINQUENCY PREVENTION ACT

The Juvenile Justice and Delinquency Prevention Act was enacted in 1974 to respond to widespread concerns about juvenile crime and the treatment of juveniles in the criminal justice system. The authors of the legislation felt that systemic reform was required. Two innovative components of the JJDP Act were the separation of adult and juvenile offenders and the removal of status offenders from secure incarceration. In addition, Section 223(a)(16) of the JJDP Act required states to "provide assurance that assistance would be available on an equitable basis to deal with all disadvantaged youth including, but not limited to, females, minority youth, mentally retarded, and emotionally or physically handicapped youth."

The next major legislative change affecting female juvenile offenders occurred in the 1977 reauthorization of the JJDP Act.[24] President Jimmy Carter requested additional funding to expand the scope of the program. The reauthorization reaffirmed congressional support for separating juveniles from adults and removing status offenders from secure settings. This action directly affected females in the juvenile justice system because, at that time, most girls who became involved with the juvenile justice system were status

---

[23] Juvenile Justice and Delinquency Prevention Act 1974, Public Law 93–415. S. 821. A bill to improve the quality of juvenile justice in the United States and to provide a comprehensive, coordinated approach to the problems of juvenile delinquency.

[24] 1977 reauthorization.

offenders. The 1975 report revealed that young females were "more likely to be referred for status offenses, i.e., conduct that would not be criminal if committed by an adult, and at a higher rate than boys referred for such conduct. Truancy, incorrigibility, and sexual delinquency are the three primary status offenses for which girls are institutionalized."

In 1988, the JJDP Act was again reauthorized[25] to focus on improving state practices and upgrading secure facilities. The overrepresentation of minorities in secure correctional settings was of particular concern. Although gender, as an issue, was referenced in the 1988 amendments, this issue was not addressed until the 1992 amendments, which required that the states prepare the following:[26]

- ❑ An analysis of gender-specific services for the prevention and treatment of juvenile delinquency.

- ❑ A plan for providing needed gender-specific services for the prevention and treatment of this population.

The 1992 amendments to the JJDP Act further echoed the 1975 report's recommendations regarding the development of gender-specific programs and funding for research and discretionary programs that would focus on female juvenile offenders.

To fulfill this congressional mandate as well as to address the recommendations of the 1975 report, OJJDP has funded gender-specific service programs and provided extensive technical assistance to state and local officials seeking to develop programs that assist female offenders and at-risk girls. OJJDP encourages and supports programs for girls that are based on a philosophical continuum of prevention, intervention, and treatment. Even with this comprehensive approach, however, many support service providers still tend to neglect and minimize the special needs of female juvenile offenders.

SPECIFIC ISSUES

Several specific issues should be addressed to complete the picture of how the juvenile justice system has responded to the female juvenile

---

[25] 1988 reauthorization.
[26] Section 223(a)(8)(B) of the Juvenile Justice and Delinquency Prevention Act of 1974 as amended.

offender in the years following the 1975 report. Likewise, specific issues should be considered to understand the factors that had a severe impact on young girls entering the juvenile justice system in 1995. In summary, any discussion of the female juvenile offender in the 1990s should include the following issues:

- ❑ Neglected program needs of female juveniles.
- ❑ Risk factors associated with female juveniles.
  - Abuse and exploitation.
  - Substance abuse.
  - Teen pregnancy and parenthood.
  - Low or damaged self-esteem.
  - Truancy and school dropout.
- ❑ Impact of risk factors.
- ❑ Effective comprehensive program strategy for girls.

NEGLECTED PROGRAM NEEDS OF FEMALE JUVENILES

According to Shay Bilchik, current OJJDP Administrator, "Our system of prevention and intervention for juveniles has traditionally been geared to the provision of services to males rather than females [who] have traditionally been ignored both at the practitioner level [and at] the academic research level."[27] Because of the limited number of girls in the system, they failed to attract significant interest in their special needs. With the prevalence of gender-related biases both in the system and in society, it was mistakenly assumed that the needs of girls could be met by the same programs that serve boys. The juvenile justice field has not institutionalized a significant number of gender-specific programs.

Contemporary studies have documented the juvenile justice system's lack of sensitivity to the gender-specific problems and the needs of girls who come into contact with the system. Additionally, a growing body of literature provides evidence that girls in the juvenile justice system are not afforded the same kinds of progressive treatment or rehabilitative opportunities that boys routinely receive.[28]

---

[27] Bilchik, Shay. 1995. Sixth Annual Workshop on Adult and Juvenile Female Offenders. Myrtle Beach, SC.
[28] Chesney-Lind, Meda and Randall G. Shelden. *Girls, Delinquency and Juvenile Justice.*

One specific practice that should be examined is bootstrapping—charging young people who have not committed a criminal offense with a delinquent offense for violation of a court order. Evidence strongly suggests that bootstrapping results in harsh and inequitable treatment of girls charged with status offenses and should only be used as a last alternative.[29] According to psychologists, society has only recently acknowledged that the girls and young women of today grow up in a world that is just beginning to understand and document their differences from men.[30, 31] Meda Chesney-Lind and Randall G. Shelden of the University of Hawaii have indicated that factors such as emotional, physical, and sexual abuse and the breakdown of the family are among the chief causes for delinquent behavior among girls.[32] Girls who have experienced these problems are at risk of becoming involved in the juvenile justice system.

Girls who enter the juvenile justice system tend to have demonstrated behavioral patterns that include running away from home, substance abuse, and suicidal tendencies. No less than 70 percent of female delinquents placed in traditional settings have been found to be victims of physical and/or sexual abuse. Nearly 80 percent have run away from home prior to incarceration.[33]

RISK FACTORS ASSOCIATED WITH FEMALE JUVENILES

To develop and implement effective prevention programs for at-risk girls and female juvenile offenders, clarification is needed of the factors that place young women at risk of involvement in the juvenile justice system.

Abuse and Exploitation

National statistics show that 8 million girls, or 1 out of every 4, are sexually abused before the age of 18. Statistics pertaining to the incidence of

---

[29] Chesney-Lind, Meda and Katherine Hunt Federle. 1992. "Special issues in juvenile justice: Gender, race, and ethnicity." In *Juvenile Justice and Public Policy: Toward a National Agenda*, ed., Ira Schwartz, pp. 165–195. New York: Macmillan.
[30] Gilligan, Carol and Lyn Mikel Brown. 1992. *Meeting At The Crossroads: Women's Psychology and Girls' Development*. Cambridge, MA: Harvard University Press.
[31] Miller, Jean Baker. 1982. *Toward A New Psychology of Women*. Boston. MA: Beacon Press.
[32] Chesney-Lind, Meda and Randall G. Shelden. *Girls, Delinquency and Juvenile Justice*.
[33] Ibid.

physical and sexual abuse and/or exploitation in the backgrounds of delinquent female juvenile offenders vary from a low of 40 percent to a high of 73 percent. Girls are much more likely than boys to be victims of sexual abuse, especially family-related abuse, and girls are more likely to report such abuse than boys.[34]

Abuse is also a primary cause for running away from home, a status offense that is often a girl's first involvement with the juvenile justice system. Studies indicate that sexually abused female runaways are more likely to engage in delinquent activities (for example, substance abuse, theft, and prostitution) than nonabused female or male runaways. According to Chesney-Lind, when seeking help, most girls seek help for the consequences rather than the causes of the abuse.[35]

Separate at-risk prevention studies conducted by Cathy Spatz Widom and Terence P. Thornberry confirm that abused children are at high risk for subsequent involvement in delinquency and violent behavior. Likewise, it is well documented that a large number of adult abusers were victims of abuse as children.[36,37] According to Widom, childhood abuse and neglect increased the likelihood of arrest as a juvenile by 53 percent, the likelihood of arrest as an adult by 38 percent, and the likelihood of committing a violent crime by 38 percent.[38] Thornberry concludes that adolescents from families experiencing more than two forms of violence are more than twice as likely to commit violent offenses as their peers from nonviolent families.[39]

In summary, the abuse and exploitation of young girls should be viewed as a major and pervasive public health threat and a primary precursor to involvement in the criminal justice system. Antiviolence initiatives should be sustained and expanded. These efforts should be supported by legislation and carried out by law enforcement agencies and the courts. Furthermore, girls' first contact with the juvenile justice system is often precipitated by their attempts to escape abuse at home. Girls need access to a continuum of placement options in which their safety can be ensured while they address the issues that brought them into the system and receive the services they will need to leave it. Many options are nonpunitive and nonsecure, including

---

[34] Ibid.
[35] Chesney-Lind, Meda. 1995. "Girls, delinquency and juvenile justice: Toward a feminist theory of young women's crime." In *The Criminal Justice System and Women*, eds., Barbara R. Price and Natalie J. Sokoloff, pp. 71–88. New York: McGraw-Hill.
[36] Widom, Cathy Spatz. 1992. *The Cycle of Violence*. NCJ 136607. Washington, DC: National Institute of Justice.
[37] Thornberry, Terence P. 1994. *Violent Families and Youth Violence*. Washington, DC: Office of Juvenile Justice and Delinquency Prevention.
[38] Widom, Cathy Spatz. *The Cycle of Violence*.
[39] Thornberry, Terence P. *Violent Families and Youth Violence*.

placement with trusted relatives or friends, foster care in private or group homes, or residential substance abuse treatment programs.

Substance Abuse

Substance abuse is another important risk factor for female juvenile delinquency. Studies report that at-risk girls often indicate that drugs allow them to escape emotional pain, which is frequently an aftermath of abuse. Over time, drug usage can become a problem or cause other problems such as addiction and the attendant behavior necessary to obtain the drugs by any possible means, including criminal activities. In 1990, the American Correctional Association (ACA) conducted a survey of female juvenile offenders in training schools and discovered that the typical female juvenile offender "started using alcohol or drugs between the ages of 12 and 15." Further, it was found that "some 64 percent used alcohol at least once or twice a week. Of the 59 percent who used cocaine, 47 percent did so on a daily basis. Similarly, of the 78 percent who used marijuana, some 47 percent did so on a daily basis."[40]

The link between drug use and sexual activity has long been known. Sexual activity among young women has steadily increased, with more than 51 percent of 15- to 19-year-olds reporting premarital sexual intercourse. According to one study, "Early initiation of sexual activity and early childbearing are associated with [alcohol and other drug use], low academic achievement, school dropout and delinquency, and pregnancy among females."[41]

Teen Pregnancy and Parenthood

The rate of teenage pregnancies in the United States is declining, according to the National Center for Health Statistics. In 1995, 57 of every 1,000 teenage girls gave birth, down from 68 per 1,000 in 1970. In 1995, an estimated 513,000 teenage girls gave birth to 13 percent of the babies born in

---

[40] American Correctional Association. 1990. *The Female Offender: What Does the Future Hold?* Lanham, MD.
[41] Bergsmann, Ilene R. "Establishing a foundation: Just the facts." In *1994 National Juvenile Female Offenders Conference: A Time For Change*, pp. 3–14. Washington, DC: Office of Juvenile Justice and Delinquency Prevention.

the United States. Teenage girls represented a third of all the unmarried mothers in the country.[42]

Teenage pregnancy and parenthood is a major delinquency risk factor for female juvenile offenders and teenage girls in general. In a study conducted by Mark Clements Research, Inc., 720 girls ages 12 to 19 were asked what would prevent pregnancy among unwed teens. The key findings are revealing.[43]

- Ninety-seven percent of the teenage girls surveyed indicated that "having parents they could talk to" could help prevent pregnancies among unmarried teens.

- Ninety-three percent said "having loving parents" reduces the risk.

- Ninety-six percent of the respondents said that "having self-respect" and "being informed about sex, pregnancy, and birth control" are critical to preventing pregnancy.

- Ninety-six percent indicated that the most influential deterrent was "being aware of the responsibility of caring for a child."

- Ninety-three percent of the girls said that "being satisfied with life would prevent teen pregnancies."[44]

Deborah Tolman, Director of the Adolescent Sexuality Project at the Center for Research on Women at Wesley College, maintains, "Girls often trade sex for love, just as they always have. Society teaches girls that love is what should matter to them, and we teach boys that what they should want most is sex. We end up shortchanging both genders."[45]

Parents are more influential than they might guess in their daughter's decision to have sex—91 percent of the girls rated their mothers and 76 percent rated their fathers as "very" or "somewhat influential." Younger teens are much more likely to view parents as important influences than older ones, unless they are victims of sexual abuse or victimization.[46]

---

[42] Adams, P.F., C.A. Schoenborn, A.J. Moss, C.W. Warren, and L. Kann. 1995. *Health-Risk Behaviors Among Our Nation's Youth: United States, 1992*. Vital and Health Statistics Series 10, No. 192; DHHS Publication No. (PHS) 95–1520. Hyattsville, MD: U.S. Department of Health and Human Services, Public Health Service, Centers for Disease Control and Prevention, National Center for Health Statistics.

[43] Chassler, Sey. 1997. "What teenage girls say about pregnancy." *Washington Post Parade Magazine*, 2 February, p. 3. Citing survey from Mark Clements Research Inc., 1996.

[44] Ibid.

[45] Ibid.

[46] Ibid.

More than 60 percent of the girls surveyed in the Clements study stated that not knowing about contraceptives or the "facts of life" was a major risk factor. The Clements study also found that, while teenage girls may be protecting themselves better in the 1990s than they did 10 years ago, contraception alone may not be enough. Emotional factors also come into play—66 percent of the girls polled said that having parents who did not give enough love and attention or having parents who did not teach morals increased the likelihood of girls becoming pregnant.[47]

Thirty-six percent of girls indicated that pregnancy occurred because of a desire "to feel needed and/or loved unconditionally"; 27 percent said that a girl might want "someone to love and care for or call her own"; and 24 percent said that a teenage girl might get pregnant to get or keep a boyfriend. Many girls reported that being pregnant was a means of obtaining love and popularity or escaping from an abusive living situation. Most female juvenile offenders see pregnancy as a response to past sexual victimization.[48]

Unfortunately, many female juvenile offenders are pregnant or are mothers when they enter the juvenile justice system. The juvenile justice system has not adequately addressed the issue of adjudicated teenage mothers. A few programs exist for pregnant girls and teenage mothers; however, they have long waiting lists and often require funding for both mother and child, a requirement that not all government agencies are willing to meet.

Low or Damaged Self-Esteem

Among female juvenile offenders, low self-esteem is another major risk factor. Girls often become involved in the juvenile justice system as truants, runaways, delinquents, and/or status offenders. Although the labels are different, common problems exist for all at-risk girls—emotional, physical, and sexual abuse and the breakdown of the family unit cause these girls to feel rejected and unloved. The majority of female juvenile offenders are victims of severely dysfunctional families and have suffered from neglect, teenage pregnancy, and violence and, as a result, are often emotionally disturbed and have limited or no self-respect.

Self-reported data show that more than half of young women in training schools have attempted suicide and 64 percent of them have tried more than

---

[47] Ibid.
[48] Ibid.

once.[49] These feelings of poor self-worth are mirrored in the larger society among teen girls as evidenced by a growing body of research in this area.[50]

Truancy and School Dropout

The typical female juvenile offender is a high school dropout. In 1990, ACA found that 27 percent of girls dropped out of school because of pregnancy and 20 percent left school to become full-time mothers.[51] Sixty-five percent of girls in training schools had completed only 1 to 3 years of high school and had not received a general equivalency diploma (GED). Of these girls, 36 percent did not return to any type of school after leaving the training school.[52]

IMPACT OF RISK FACTORS

The connection between risk factors (abuse and exploitation, substance abuse, teen pregnancy and parenthood, low or damaged self-esteem, and truancy and school dropout) and delinquency has an immense impact on determining whether at-risk girls and female juvenile offenders will become successful and productive women in society or become incarcerated offenders both as juveniles and as adults.

A 1996 study completed by Leslie Acoca and James Austin on incarcerated women in California, Connecticut, and Florida found that a significant proportion of the women in the study reported that they had been in trouble as girls and yet little or nothing had been done to help them. The study found that:

❑ Forty-six percent of women were first arrested when they were 17 years of age or younger (in Connecticut, 56 percent of the women were first arrested as juveniles). In addition, 15.5 percent of the women reported that they had lived in at least one foster home while growing up.

---

[49] American Correctional Association. *The Female Offender: What Does the Future Hold?*
[50] Chesney-Lind, Meda and Randall G. Shelden. *Girls, Delinquency and Juvenile Justice.*
[51] American Correctional Association. *The Female Offender: What Does the Future Hold?*
[52] Ibid.

- Nearly half of the women (48.3 percent) had been suspended or expelled from school, and more than 25 percent had either required a special class in school or repeated a grade.
- More than half of the women (56.3 percent) ran away from home as girls, often to escape abuse. Girls were most likely to be expelled from school, run away from home, or be placed in a foster home between the ages of 12 and 13.[53] When asked specific questions about their entry into and involvement with the juvenile justice system, women in the study indicated the following:
- More than one in four (26.7 percent) reported that their involvement with the juvenile justice system started with being labeled status offenders (most commonly for running away from home), declared delinquent by a juvenile court (26.8 percent), or placed on juvenile probation (28.9 percent). Nearly one in three (32.6 percent) stated that they had been locked up in a juvenile detention center for more than 1 day.
- As juveniles more than one in four were either placed in special classes or held back a grade in school. Of those who were placed in special classes, the highest percentage were placed in classes for children with learning and perceptual difficulties.
- Nearly half reported that, as juveniles, they had been suspended or expelled or both. Although 27.5 percent of the women experienced their first serious school failure at age 8 or 9, the median age at which girls were likely to be first expelled or suspended was 13.[54]

The Acoca and Austin report noted that early adolescence was the age at which those interviewed were at the highest risk for school failure, running away, and out-of-home placement. A majority of the women (56.3 percent) ran away from home at least once when they were children. Of the women who ran away as girls, 28.7 percent cited the desire for more freedom, 24.1 percent cited the need to escape abuse at home, and 14.9 percent cited the feeling that they were not wanted at home as their primary reason for running away. This report indicated that the median age that the women first ran away as girls was 13.[55]

---

[53] Acoca, Leslie and James Austin. 1996. "The crisis: Women in prison." Draft report submitted to the Charles E. Culpeper Foundation. San Francisco, CA: National Council on Crime and Delinquency.
[54] Ibid.
[55] Ibid.

In studying these incarcerated women, the researchers found that a history of abuse is a common characteristic of women in prison. One of the goals of the Acoca and Austin study was to identify the time in the women's lives when the abuse occurred. To this end, each woman was asked a set of 32 concrete and specific questions about emotional, physical, and sexual harm that she might have experienced as a child (17 and under) or as an adult (18 and older). Their responses indicated the following.

- Most of the women (72.2 percent) reported that they had experienced one or more forms of emotional abuse, and 67.5 percent reported that they had experienced one or more forms of physical or sexual abuse, as children.

- Some of the women (31.1 percent) reported that they had been raped or sodomized as children. Of this group, a small percentage (11.3 percent) also indicated that they were victimized more than five times or repeatedly.

- Forty-five percent of the women reported having been beaten or physically abused in another way as children, and 35.8 percent who reported this type of physical abuse experienced it more than five times.[56]

This study, along with others, documents the importance of establishing comprehensive gender-specific services for at-risk girls and female juvenile offenders to prevent their entry into or return to the criminal justice system.

EFFECTIVE COMPREHENSIVE PROGRAM STRATEGY FOR GIRLS

Myriad social and emotional issues and risk factors are involved with female juvenile offenders in the juvenile justice system. Despite the multiplicity of their problems, however, female juvenile offenders and at-risk girls respond positively when placed in a caring environment. To address the needs of this population, it is necessary to develop and implement innovative community-based programs that provide comprehensive, gender-specific prevention, treatment, and rehabilitative care that includes case management and followup for at-risk and delinquent

---

[56] Ibid.

girls.[57] An effective comprehensive strategy for this population should include the following:

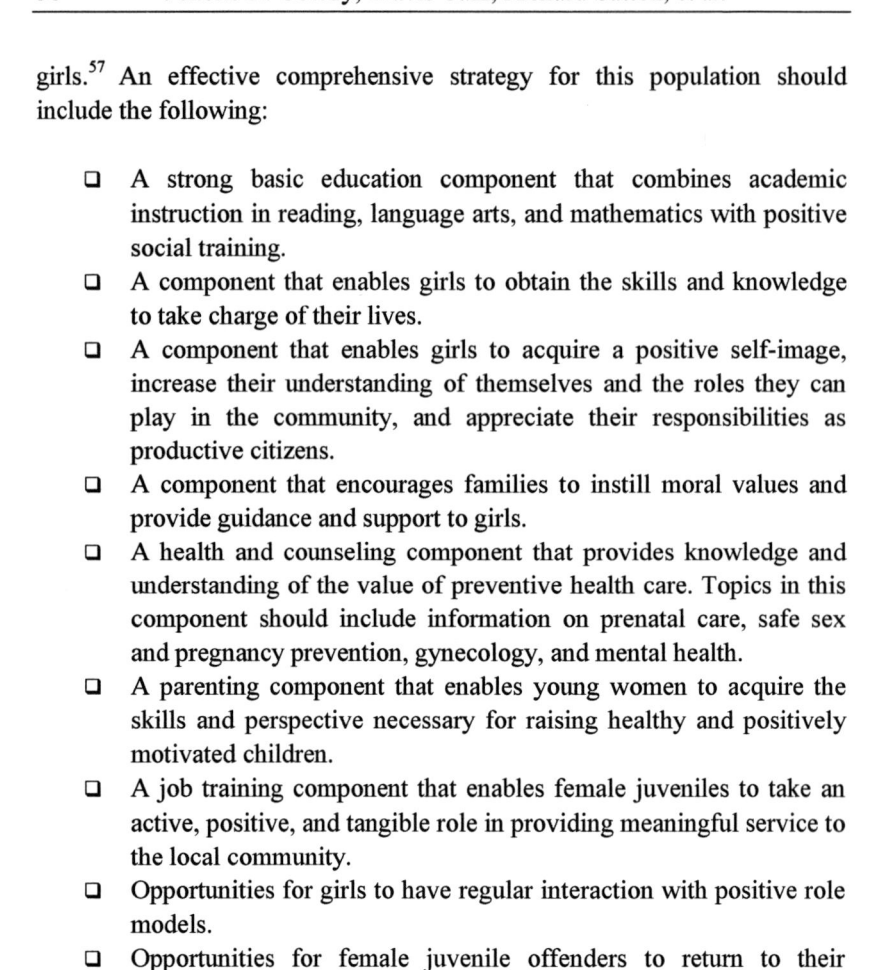

- A strong basic education component that combines academic instruction in reading, language arts, and mathematics with positive social training.
- A component that enables girls to obtain the skills and knowledge to take charge of their lives.
- A component that enables girls to acquire a positive self-image, increase their understanding of themselves and the roles they can play in the community, and appreciate their responsibilities as productive citizens.
- A component that encourages families to instill moral values and provide guidance and support to girls.
- A health and counseling component that provides knowledge and understanding of the value of preventive health care. Topics in this component should include information on prenatal care, safe sex and pregnancy prevention, gynecology, and mental health.
- A parenting component that enables young women to acquire the skills and perspective necessary for raising healthy and positively motivated children.
- A job training component that enables female juveniles to take an active, positive, and tangible role in providing meaningful service to the local community.
- Opportunities for girls to have regular interaction with positive role models.
- Opportunities for female juvenile offenders to return to their families; when this is not possible, establishment of an alternative plan such as therapeutic foster care or supported independent living.
- Child care services for girls who are mothers.[58, 59]

The multiservice needs of the female juvenile offender can be met through a community's use of OJJDP's Comprehensive Strategy for Serious, Violent, and Chronic Juvenile Offenders, which emphasizes the integration of services and the need for organizations to collaborate in the creation of a

---

[57] Schwartz, Ira M. and Frank Orlando. 1991. *Programming for Young Women in the Juvenile Justice System*. Ann Arbor, MI: Center for the Study of Youth Policy.
[58] Ibid.
[59] Weiss, Faedra L., Heather Johnston Nicholson, and Maria Magdalena Cretella. 1996. *Prevention and Parity: Girls in Juvenile Justice*. NCJ 161868. Indianapolis, IN: Girls Incorporated.

continuum-of-care system. OJJDP recognizes that a comprehensive approach to delinquency prevention and intervention requires collaboration between the juvenile justice system and other service provision systems, including mental health, health, child welfare, and education. Developing mechanisms that effectively link these different service providers at the program level should be an important component of every community's plan to provide gender-specific services. In addition, local efforts should be supported by a highly visible national girl's initiative. Such an initiative should not only support program implementation, but also support program evaluation and female-specific research. It is far easier and less costly in both monetary and labor terms to develop community-based demonstration programs to prevent problems before they occur or to intervene with proven effective approaches as soon as they are discovered than to wait until a girl is in serious trouble.[60, 61]

CONCLUSION

Young women require access to a wide variety of programs and placements to address their specific needs, such as drug addiction, learning disabilities, teen pregnancy, motherhood, and histories of abuse. Substance abuse programs specifically designed for girls are in short supply. In addition, there are few programs for pregnant and parenting girls in the juvenile justice system,[62] and many of the best programs accept teen mothers for treatment only if they place their children in the custody of another individual.

Misguided stereotypes and inadequate programming continue because there is a lack of information on female juvenile offenders. Research on juvenile offenders should include significant samples of girls, when possible, to identify and address the impact of gender on girls' life situations, behaviors, strengths, and needs. To prevent girls from becoming involved in the juvenile justice system, profiles of girls who are likely to become involved in the system should be identified. Efforts to predict which young

---

[60] Wilson, John J. and James C. Howell. 1993. *Comprehensive Strategy for Serious, Violent, and Chronic Juvenile Offenders: Program Summary.* NCJ 143453. Washington, DC: Office of Juvenile Justice and Delinquency Prevention.
[61] Howell, James C., ed., 1995. *Guide for Implementing the Comprehensive Strategy for Serious, Violent, and Chronic Juvenile Offenders.* Washington, DC: Office of Juvenile Justice and Delinquency Prevention.
[62] Bergsmann, Ilene R. "Establishing a foundation: Just the facts." In *1994 National Juvenile Female Offenders Conference: A Time For Change.*

people are likely to engage in at-risk or delinquent behavior, based on early childhood behavior, have proved to be of little success for girls. Therefore, important factors for predicting female juvenile offenders' behavior (for example, a history of abuse) should be included in models.[63] Further investigations of risk and protective factors that either place girls at risk for juvenile delinquency or shield them from it are needed along with further clarification of the difference between the needs and characteristics of male and female juvenile offenders.

Research programs that focus on the increase in juvenile female violent crime, more active roles being played by female offenders in gangs, and possible inequitable treatment in the juvenile justice system of girls who are members of a minority group are needed to educate juvenile justice system practitioners.[64]

In developing programs and services for the female juvenile offender, juvenile justice policymakers and practitioners need to remember that for many girls who are involved in the juvenile justice system, delinquent behavior is likely to be a response to the terrible circumstances in which they often find themselves. The behavior reflects their deep need and unspoken desire to be understood, to be encouraged, and to be given positive direction in a world which, for many of them, can seem quite confusing. Juvenile justice policymakers and practitioners should be committed to the proposition that an effective juvenile justice system is one that is highly responsive to the needs of the juvenile population, regardless of gender.

The best interventions are those that strengthen families and help parents access skills and resources to raise their children in a safe and nurturing home and community. These interventions should begin early and include both families and individual children. However, well-designed interventions can also have an effect on girls who are already involved in the juvenile justice system.[65, 66] Programs should be designed that address risk factors for female juveniles and deal with all stages of delinquency from prevention to early intervention to aftercare.

The juvenile justice system is based on prevention, intervention, and treatment; therefore, meaningful preventive measures, successful intervention efforts, and constructive rehabilitative programs should remain

---

[63] Weiss, Faedra L., Heather Johnston Nicholson, and Maria Magdalena Cretella. 1996. *Prevention and Parity: Girls in Juvenile Justice*. Indianapolis, IN: Girls Incorporated.
[64] Ibid.
[65] Ibid.
[66] Marcia R. Chaiken. 1995. "Evaluation of the Girls Incorporated Connections Advocacy Activities: Advances for Sound Adolescent Development." Executive Summary. Alexandria, VA: LINC.

at the heart of the system. The system should both hold offenders accountable and nurture them. This is particularly true for juvenile female offenders in light of the deep emotional needs evidenced by many young women who are in the system. Likewise, an effective juvenile justice system is one that promotes and fosters self-control and responsibility among young women, helps them become accountable for their actions, and promotes the public safety and welfare. Juvenile justice policymakers and practitioners should be certain that these principles are part of the juvenile justice system in all cities, regions, and states. The challenge for federal, state, and local agencies is to provide resources, training, and technical assistance to satisfactorily accomplish this goal.

RECOMMENDATIONS FROM THE OJP COORDINATION GROUP ON WOMEN

1. Continue research focusing specifically on girls and demonstration programs that include girls.
2. Create more alternatives to abusive home situations.
3. Reduce inequitable treatment of female juveniles while tailoring state and local programs to meet the needs of girls.
4. Examine the practice of bootstrapping juvenile female offenders.
5. Promote gender-specific interventions.
6. Focus on state and local risk-based and early intervention strategies for female offenders.
7. Develop and implement continuum-of-care programs for girls in communities nationwide.
8. Ensure that traditional and nontraditional career options are available to female juveniles.
9. Empower young women and prepare them for productive futures through prevention, treatment, and intervention programs.
10. Support model demonstration programs that focus specifically on the needs of female juvenile offenders. Evaluate these model programs and disseminate the results.
11. Support local efforts through a highly visible national girls' initiative.

Chapter 3

WOMEN AND GIRLS AS VICTIMS

INTRODUCTION

The year 1975 was important for both the Law Enforcement Assistance Administration (LEAA) and the crime victims movement. The LEAA Task Force on Women was visionary in that, in its study, *The Report of the LEAA Task Force on Women* (hereafter referred to as the 1975 report), it recommended an indepth analysis of female crime victims to ascertain whether the characteristics of victimization for men were different from those for women. For the crime victims movement, the nationwide coordination of victim services became possible with the formation of the National Organization for Victim Assistance (NOVA). Subsequently, the nation witnessed the establishment of sexual assault treatment centers, domestic violence programs, child abuse prevention and treatment services, hundreds of Mothers Against Drunk Driving chapters, and numerous Parents of Murdered Children groups. For the most part, these services were founded by women. In the United States, these groups and other powerful voices were working to enact a crime victim bill of rights, constitutional amendments, and other enabling statutes to serve all crime victims, and most often were championed by women and on behalf of women.[*]

Supporting the explosion of interest in assisting victims of crime was the 1982 President's Task Force on Victims of Crime and the 1984 Attorney General's Task Force on Family Violence. *The Final Report of the President's Task Force on Victims of Crime,* along with other documents,

---

[*] For more information on the history of the battered women's movement, please see Susan Schechter's book, *Women and Male Violence,* published by South End Press.

led the way for the passage of the Victims of Crime Act (VOCA) in 1984, which established the Office for Victims of Crime (OVC) in the U.S. Department of Justice (DOJ) and the Crime Victims Fund. The Crime Victims Fund garners fines paid by federal offenders to be passed on to the states for victim compensation and assistance services and to enhance services to victims of federal crimes. In 1997, more than $471 million from federal offenders was distributed to the states. Federal laws were amended in 1996 to include expanded rights and assistance to federal crime victims.

More recently, the Violent Crime Control and Law Enforcement Act of 1994 included the Violence Against Women Act (VAWA), which provided additional rights to victims of stalking, domestic violence, and sexual assault, and created a formula and two discretionary grant programs administered by the Office of Justice Programs (OJP), Violence Against Women Grants Office (VAWGO). In FY 1995, Congress authorized $26 million for STOP (Services, Training, Officers, Prosecutors) Violence Against Women formula grant awards to states and tribal governments. Also in 1995, OVC provided approximately $3 million in discretionary grant money to identify "promising practices" and to improve victim services. In FY 1996, Congress authorized $130 million for STOP grants and additional funds for two discretionary programs—$7 million to the Rural Domestic Violence and Child Victimization Enforcement Grant Program and $28 million to Grants To Encourage Arrest Policies. In FY 1998, $172 million was appropriated for STOP grants, including $145 million in direct formula grant awards to all states and territories.[1]

A program that benefits all crime victims but is of particular interest to female victims of crime is the Bureau of Prison's (BOP's) Victim Witness Program, which notifies victims of an adult offender's placement in a community, escape from incarceration, release from confinement, or death. The notification includes a form that details the offender's current location, parole eligibility date (if applicable), or date of release or death. Victims also receive a contact name and telephone number to call should they have questions about the offender's status. BOP continues these efforts until the offender is released from BOP custody or until a victim or witness no longer wishes to be notified. Some states, such as Kentucky, have implemented similar programs.

---

[1] U.S. Department of Justice. 1997. *Office of Justice Programs Annual Report, Fiscal Year 1997*. Washington, DC.

THEN AND NOW: A REVIEW OF ISSUES AND PROGRESS

The 1975 report made three recommendations regarding female victimization:

1. Fund a research grant to fully analyze the nature and characteristics of female victimization, utilizing the National Crime Panel Survey (also known as the National Crime Victimization Survey, which is administered by the Bureau of Justice Statistics) and other sources of relevant data.
2. Develop and administer supplemental questions to the National Crime Panel Survey to collect data regarding topics relevant to female victimization, especially on the treatment of male and female victims of crime by the criminal justice system.
3. Develop a new agency initiative aimed at innovative service for female victims of crime with an appropriate level of funding if data analysis indicates that female victims have special needs.

The first two recommendations addressed data collection and the third suggested allocating additional resources to service female victims of crime. Unfortunately, 20 years later we are still asking some of the same questions and making the same recommendations. Even though the National Crime Victimization Survey now provides data on women, some researchers think the age group surveyed should be lowered to crime victims age 12 and under. As the *Rape in America* report showed, the most frequently victimized groups are preteens and adolescent girls.[2] The 1995 Office of Juvenile Justice and Delinquency Prevention (OJJDP) publication, *Juvenile Offenders and Victims: A National Report,* also indicates that adolescents are the age group most likely to be victimized.[3] However, gender differences are discussed in the document only in a cursory fashion, primarily as they relate to homicide. It appears that age 12 was selected because of the assumption that crimes against younger children would fall under child abuse reporting. However, as the OJJDP report demonstrates, many children are the victims of homicide, robbery, assault, rape, and other crimes that would not be

---

[2] Kilpatrick, Dean G., Christine N. Edmunds, and Anne Seymour. 1992. *Rape in America: A Report to the Nation.* Arlington, VA: National Victim Center.

[3] Snyder, Howard N. and Melissa Sickmund. 1995. *Juvenile Offenders and Victims: A National Report.* Washington, DC: Office of Juvenile Justice and Delinquency Prevention.

included in the child abuse reporting requirements unless the crimes were committed by a family member or caretaker.

Some could argue that funds for the Victims of Crime Act help to address the third recommendation in the 1975 report—the creation of an agency designed to provide specialized services for female victims of crime.[4] It is true that a substantial amount of the money allocated by VOCA funds programs serve women and children. In addition, as a result of Title V of the Violent Crime Control and Law Enforcement Act of 1994, the Violence Against Women Act, the Violence Against Women Office (VAWO), and the Violence Against Women Grants Office were created.[5] Subsequently, a number of grant programs have been developed to increase and enhance services for female crime victims.

In the early 1980s, only five states had crime victims bills of rights. Today, 48 states have crime victims bill of rights, 29 have crime victim constitutional amendments, and all 50 states have some references to crime victim rights throughout their statutes. Unfortunately, many of these rights are not afforded to the victims of juvenile offenders. This is gradually changing, however, and even the OJJDP report *Combating Violence and Delinquency: The National Juvenile Justice Action Plan* called for the enactment of victim rights in the juvenile justice system.[6] In the federal system, the Victim and Witness Protection Act was signed in 1982 and the Victims' Rights and Restitution Act became law in 1990. In 1996, the Clinton administration sponsored legislation to revise federal statutes to ensure that victims of juvenile offenders would have the same rights as they would have if the offender was an adult.[7] On April 22, 1996, a U.S. constitutional amendment was introduced to provide equal rights for the victims of crime across the nation.[8]

Currently, more than 3,000 crime victim assistance programs are funded by VOCA and all states have a compensation program to assist with medical

---

[4] Victims of Crime Act of 1984, 42 USC §10601.

[5] Violence Against Women Act, Violent Crime Control and Law Enforcement Act of 1994, Pub. L. No. 103:322, § 2001 (b(6)).

[6] Coordinating Council on Juvenile Justice and Delinquency Prevention. 1996. *Combating Violence and Delinquency: The National Juvenile Justice Action Plan*. Washington, DC: Office of Juvenile Justice and Delinquency Prevention.

[7] Antigang and Youth Violence Control Act of 1996. Introduction pending Clinton administration proposal.

[8] Kyl, Jon, Dianne Feinstein, and Henry Hyde. *Victims Bill of Rights Constitutional Amendment*, SJR 52/HJR 174. Introduced April 22, 1996. 104th Congress, 2d Session.

bills, funeral bills, and counseling.[9] However, the compensation funds are not always available to the victims of juvenile offenders.

Even the terminology has changed since 1975. The word *victim* is now often replaced by the more positive *survivor* to note the power of having adjusted to an event. *Wife-beating*, a phrase used in the 1975 report, is now encompassed in the broader topic of *family violence,* since violence in the home affects other family members in addition to wives. The term *victim* is not limited to the persons harmed directly by a crime but also includes their family members, friends, and community. Exhibit 3–1 provides a comparison of services for victims of crime in 1975 and 1998.

Despite this progress, a number of issues pertaining to female victims of crime remain to be addressed. Four major female crime victim issues have been identified in 1998:

- Basic concerns of crime victims.
- Women as victims in the general population.
- Adult female offenders as victims.
- Staff victimization.

BASIC CONCERNS OF CRIME VICTIMS

Crime victims are now beginning to receive basic rights in the criminal justice system, including:

- The right to information about the offender's case, disposition, sentence, and release.
- The right to provide an impact statement to the court, the presentence investigator, and the parole board.
- The right to participate in all proceedings in which the offender may participate.
- The right to receive services and restitution.

---

[9] Office for Victims of Crime. 1998. *State Crime Victim Compensation and Assistance Grant Programs.* Washington, DC: U.S. Department of Justice.

Exhibit 3–1
Accomplishments for Crime Victims Between 1970 and 1998

1970
- No victim bills of rights or constitutional amendments.
- Few victim-witness programs or crime victim compensation funds at the state or federal level.
- No national organizations to assist crime victims and their survivors.
- No organizations for people who survive homicide victims.
- No discussion of domestic violence at the national level.
- No discussion of sexual assault victims at the national level.
- No organization working to change the laws on drunk driving or to assist the victims of these crashes.
- No corrections-based victim services.
- No programs to address staff as crime victims.
- No programs for offenders to take responsibility for their crimes or the long-term impact of their crimes on their victims.

1998
- Forty-eight state bills of rights introduced and 29 state constitutions amended.
- Federal Victim/Witness Protection Act enacted. First victim compensation program started in 1965; others started in early 1970s. Victims of Crime Act enacted in 1984.
- The National Organization for Victim Assistance formed in 1975 and the National Victim Center formed in 1982.
- Parents of Murdered Children founded in 1978—now with thousands of members and many similar support groups, most started by women.
- Thousands of programs established to serve domestic violence victims and the children who witness such violence. The 1994 Violence Against Women Act enacted and the Violence Against Women Grant Office established.
- Hundreds of rape treatment programs established, and training has been improved for law enforcement, medical, and legal personnel to help these victims.
- Mothers Against Drunk Driving, started by a woman, now has thousands of members, has been active in changing hundreds of laws, and claims to have saved thousands of lives.
- Many departments of corrections implemented victim service programs based on the OVC-sponsored Victims and Corrections Grant in 1991.
- Staff crime victims addressed as part of the Victims and Corrections Project.
- The Impact of Crime on Victims classes started in 1985 and are now replicated in about 15 states.

All states now have some type of victim compensation and assistance provision. Most of the rights pertain to law enforcement, the courts, and the prosecutor. However, in some states, corrections departments do not have the statutory authority to offer victim services. Even when victims rights are recognized, they may not be enforced and there are few sanctions for failure.

One such case in which a victim's rights were not enforced occurred in Kentucky, when a victim requested notification of the release of an offender and did not receive it. Mary Byron, of Jeffersontown, Kentucky, was killed by her estranged boyfriend Donovan Harris on her 21st birthday in December 1993, less than 3 weeks after he had been charged with raping her at gunpoint. At the time she was murdered, she did not know that Donovan had been released from jail on bond because Jeffersontown Detective Robert Perkins failed to notify her as she had requested.[10] Byron's estate sued the Jeffersontown Police Department and Detective Perkins, but the suit was dismissed. Byron's estate filed an appeal, but the appellate court ruled that the city of Jeffersontown and the detective did not have an obligation to notify Byron of Harris' release.[11]

Another concern for crime victims is self-blame, wherein the victim feels some responsibility for the crime's occurrence. This concern was addressed in the 1975 report, which stated, "The system's response tends to focus less on the injury and sensitive treatment of the victim, and more on evaluating the victim's credibility." The training of crime victim services personnel should address sensitivity toward crime victims' feelings of self-blame.

Victims also have an interest in preventing future victimization. To address this concern, all correctional facilities should require offender participation in an Impact of Crime on Victims course. Offenders should be held accountable for the harm they have caused and recognize the impact that their crimes have had on their victims. These offender awareness efforts have been implemented in California, New York, Ohio, Pennsylvania, and Washington state, as well as every military correctional facility in the country, and are regarded as being highly successful.[12]

---

[10] "Notifying Victim Not Officer's Duty, Court Upholds Suit Dismissal, Says City, Police Not At Fault." *Lexington Herald-Leader,* July 13, 1996. p. C4.
[11] Victim Information and Notification Everyday (VINE). 1995. Automated Victim Notification Services. Louisville, KY.
[12] California Youth Authority. 1996. *Today Special Edition.* Sacramento, CA.

WOMEN AS VICTIMS IN THE GENERAL POPULATION

The 1975 report indicates that, although rape victims received a great deal of public attention at that time, little attention had been directed toward girls and women who were victims of other types of assault, particularly assaults occurring in the home. The report recognized that victims of rape were often victimized twice; initially by the rapist and subsequently by the criminal justice system in its handling of the offense. Since 1975, greater attention has been devoted toward violence against women and the attendant criminal justice system's response. Greater public awareness of violent crimes that are committed primarily against women (e.g., domestic violence, sexual assault, and stalking) has led to some statutory changes and has triggered innovative approaches at all levels of government to reduce such crimes. Since the 1975 report was published, OJP has embarked upon numerous research and/or demonstration projects to advance knowledge in this area and to help criminal justice agencies develop effective strategies to improve their response to the violence many women face every day. Examples of these efforts can be found in *A Report to the Assistant Attorney General,* which was developed by the OJP Family Violence Working Group.[13]

Areas in which the criminal justice community has focused on improving its response to crimes against women and girls include domestic violence, sexual assault, stalking, juvenile victimization, and elderly victimization.

Domestic Violence

Domestic and family violence received little attention and rarely received an adequate or appropriate criminal justice response in 1975. The criminal justice system's inattention to domestic violence was due to a host of different factors. These factors included but were not limited to:

- ❑ Statutorial limitations.
- ❑ Unwillingness of the criminal justice system to treat domestic violence as a crime commensurate to violence against a stranger.

---

[13] Office of Justice Programs Family Violence Working Group. 1997. *A Report to the Assistant Attorney General.* Washington, DC: U.S. Department of Justice.

❑ Lack of cooperation from the victim in the legal process.
❑ Confusion regarding the role of the criminal justice system in addressing domestic violence.

In the past, police officers were limited by statutes in 22 states; these states allowed officers to make an arrest in misdemeanor domestic violence cases *only* if they witnessed the violent episode.[14] Unfortunately, most cases of domestic violence were classified as misdemeanors. Furthermore, and perhaps most important, police officers realized that few domestic violence cases would ultimately result in prosecution. Because victims of domestic violence are psychologically and economically involved with the offender, they are more likely to voluntarily dismiss complaints. Prosecutors and judges tended to treat such charges lightly because of the relationships between victims and offenders.[15]

As with the police, prosecutors historically were faulted for not treating domestic and family violence cases seriously, failing to file charges in cases presented by the police, or discouraging willing victims from pursuing criminal complaints. Prosecutors were disinclined to pursue convictions in domestic violence cases primarily because of evidentiary problems, the lack of cooperation of many victims to move forward with prosecution, concerns about family privacy, or an unwillingness to prosecute with meaningful sanctions.[16, 17]

The court system also had not treated domestic violence cases as seriously as it had addressed other violence cases involving strangers. Domestic violence cases often were assigned a lower priority for prosecution and punishment, and the sanctions applied to nonfelonious intimate violence cases often were minor. In addition, women were prevented from acquiring legal remedies due to legal barriers. Prior to the late 1970s, women could not obtain a restraining order against a violent husband unless they were prepared to file for a divorce.[18] When protective orders were made available,

---

[14] Lerman, Lisa and Francis Livingston. 1983. "State legislation on domestic violence." *Response* 4:1–19.
[15] Lincoln, Alan J. and Murray A. Straus. 1985. *Crime and the Family.* Springfield, IL: Thomas Books.
[16] Elliott, Delbert. 1989. "Criminal justice procedures in family violence crimes." In Vol. 11 of *Crime and Justice: An Annual Review of Research. Family Violence*, eds. L. Ohlin and M. Tonry, pp. 427–480. Chicago, IL: University of Chicago Press.
[17] Ford, David A. 1993. *The Indianapolis Domestic Violence Prosecution Experiment: Final Report.* National Institute of Justice Research Project, Grant 86–IJ–CX–0012. Indianapolis, IN: Indiana University.
[18] U.S. Commission on Civil Rights. January 1982. *Under the Rule of Thumb: Battered Women and the Administration of Justice.* Washington, DC.

they were seldom enforced, their use in emergencies was difficult, and sanctions for violations were minimal.

Responses to domestic violence began to change in the late 1960s. As a result of the work of feminist activists, rape crisis counselors, and researchers working with women, domestic violence or violence toward intimate partners was raised as a social problem within the context of violence against women.[19] LEAA took the lead in fostering a broad response to this issue. Twenty-three programs were funded for various services including shelters, treatment programs for wife beaters, special prosecution units, mediation units, and civil legal interventions between 1976 and 1981.[20]

Changes in criminal justice practices regarding domestic violence were reflected in legal statutes. During the 1970s, 47 states passed domestic violence legislation requiring changes in protection orders, authorizing warrantless arrests for misdemeanor domestic assault, and recognizing a history of abuse and threat as a legal defense for women who killed their abusive husbands.

The Minneapolis Domestic Violence Experiment

The shift in police response to domestic violence in the 1980s from counseling/mediation to carrying out arrests is partly attributable to the results of the Minneapolis Domestic Violence Experiment.[21] This study found that the prevalence of subsequent domestic violence was reduced by nearly 50 percent when the suspect was arrested. Not only was the Minneapolis Domestic Violence Experiment instrumental in prompting police departments nationwide to adopt pro-arrest policies, it also paved the way for six replications and extensions of the Minneapolis experiment collectively known as the Spouse Assault Replication Program (SARP). These studies were conducted by the following U.S. police departments: Colorado Springs, Colorado; Miami (Metro-Dade County), Florida; Atlanta, Georgia; Omaha, Nebraska; Charlotte, North Carolina; and Milwaukee, Wisconsin. These projects were funded by the National Institute of Justice (NIJ).

The replications and extensions of the Minneapolis experiment produced inconsistent results. Either no deterrent effect of arrest on subsequent violence was found or only certain types of offenders were deterred. In the

---

[19] Fagan, Jeffrey. 1996. *The Criminalization of Domestic Violence: Promises and Limits.* Research Report. Washington, DC: National Institute of Justice.
[20] Ibid., p. 7.
[21] Sherman, Lawrence A. and Richard A. Berk. 1984. *The Minneapolis Domestic Violence Experiment.* Police Foundation Reports, No. 1. Washington, DC: Police Foundation.

worst cases, an arrest escalated the violence. The studies strongly suggest the need for a corollary response from prosecutors and judges if the efforts of police are to be successful. In other words, for an arrest to be an effective domestic violence intervention, it should be part of a coordinated and integrated response to the problem on the part of the entire criminal justice system.

The Indianapolis Domestic Violence Experiment

In addition to research assessing the effects of various police responses to domestic violence, NIJ has also funded research on the impact of prosecution on the control or reoccurrence of domestic assault. One of the most comprehensive prosecution studies was the Indianapolis Domestic Violence Experiment.[22, 23] The results of this study showed no significant deterrent effect from traditional prosecution. However, there was a significant decrease in severe violence when victim-initiated prosecutorial actions were compared with the traditional prosecutorial procedures. When victims threatened to prosecute and then followed through with prosecution, offenders were more likely to be deterred than those offenders whose victims did not follow through with prosecution or who were prosecuted under traditional procedures. These findings suggest that the threat of prosecution, coupled with prosecution, may be used to empower victims of domestic violence.

Other Federal Initiatives

Other initiatives at the federal level were prompted by the 1984 report of the Attorney General's Task Force on Family Violence. The report recommended coordinated community responses to domestic violence, rewriting applicable laws, and reforming the operations of the justice system. NIJ currently has intramural research efforts under way to examine the relationship between domestic violence and homicide. The Bureau of Justice Assistance (BJA) funded family violence demonstration programs in 11 jurisdictions to establish interagency coordinating committees.[24, 25]

---

[22] Ford, David A. 1991. "Prosecution as a power source: A note on empowering women in violent conjugal relationships." *Law and Society Review* 25:313–334.
[23] Ford, David A. 1993. *The Indianapolis Domestic Violence Prosecution Experiment: Final Report*. Indianapolis, IN: Indiana University.
[24] Harrell, Adele V., Janice A. Roel, and Kathryn A. Kapsak. 1988. *Family Violence Intervention Demonstration Programs Evaluation.* Vol. II of *Case Studies*. Bureau of Justice Assistance Report. Washington, DC: Institute of Social Analysis.
[25] Bureau of Justice Assistance. 1993. *Family Violence: Interventions for the Justice System.* Program Brief. Washington, DC: U.S. Department of Justice.

Future Implication for Criminal Justice Response

Despite changes in the criminal justice system's response to domestic violence, current data demonstrate the need for a coordinated and integrated approach to reduce and prevent domestic violence (see exhibit 3–2). Such an approach suggests a partnership among law enforcement, prosecution, the courts, and victim advocates and service providers. For the criminal justice system response to be effective, professionals in the various components of the system need to have a shared vision that prioritizes the safety and well-being of the victim.

Exhibit 3–2
Domestic Violence Statistics

- According to estimates from the redesigned National Crime Victimization Survey, females age 12 or older experienced nearly 5 million violent victimizations in 1992 and 1993. More than 75 percent of these victims knew or were related to their attacker, and injuries occurred more often when the offender was an intimate.[26]
- Approximately 2 million women are severely assaulted by male partners each year.[27]
- Women are six times more likely than men to experience violence committed by an intimate.[28]
- Twenty-six percent of all female murder victims in 1995 were slain by husbands or intimate partners.[29]

Sexual Assault

As with domestic violence, sexual assault statistics further demonstrate the need for a systemic response to combat this form of violence against women (see exhibit 3–3).

---

[26] Bachman, Ronet and Linda E. Saltzman. 1995. *Violence Against Women: Estimates from the Redesigned Survey.* Bureau of Justice Statistics Special Report. Washington, DC: U.S. Department of Justice.
[27] Brown, R. 1992. "Violence against women: Relevance for medical practitioners." *Journal of the American Medical Association* 267(23):3184–3189. Washington, DC: Council on Scientific Affairs, American Medical Association.
[28] Bachman, Ronet and Linda E. Saltzman. *Violence Against Women: Estimates from the Redesigned Survey.*
[29] Uniform Crime Reports Division, Federal Bureau of Investigations. 1996. *Crime in the United States, 1995.* Washington, DC.

> **Exhibit 3–3**
> **Sexual Assault Statistics**
>
> ❑ Every year approximately 683,000 adult women are forcibly raped.[30]
> ❑ By 1992, at least 12.1 million women had been the victim of rape at some point in their lives.[31]
> ❑ The National Women's Study found that 75 percent of rapes were committed by an acquaintance, relative, intimate, or husband of the victim.[32]
> ❑ Only 16 percent of rapes are ever reported to the police.[33]
> ❑ Fifteen percent of the women in a nationally representative sample of female college students had experienced acquaintance rape; the average age of the victim was 18. For at least 41 percent of these women, a sexual assault was their first sexual experience.[34] Almost 90 percent of these victims did not report the offense to the police.[35]

The history of sexual assault parallels that of domestic violence in regard to statutory limitations and the lack of an adequate criminal justice response. Until the 1970s, most state sexual assault laws required:

❑ Prompt reporting, which barred a victim's delayed criminal report.
❑ Corroboration by other witnesses.
❑ Resistance, which required the victim to physically resist the attacker.

These statutory requirements limited the number of domestic violence cases that were reported. By the mid-1980s, however, nearly all states had enacted laws that treated rape like other crimes (see exhibit 3–4). These laws focused on the unlawful act of the offender and did not concentrate on the behavior of the victim.

---

[30] Kilpatrick, Dean G., Christine N. Edmunds, and Anne Seymour. *Rape in America: A Report to the Nation.*
[31] Ibid.
[32] National Institute on Drug Abuse, National Victim Center, and Crime Victims Research and Treatment Center. 1992. *The National Women's Study.* Arlington, VA: National Victim Center.
[33] Kilpatrick, Dean G., Christine N. Edmunds, and Anne Seymour. *Rape in America: A Report to the Nation.*
[34] Koss, Mary P. 1988. "Hidden rape: Sexual aggression and victimization in a national sample in higher education." In *Rape and Sexual Assault II*, ed. A.W. Burgess, 3–25. New York, NY: Garland.
[35] Adams, A. and G. Abarbanel. 1988. *Sexual Assault on Campus: What Colleges Can Do?* Santa Monica, CA: Santa Monica Hospital Rape Treatment Center.

> **Exhibit 3–4**
> **Changes in Sexual Assault Statutes**
>
> ❑ Rape is now more broadly defined to include any type of sexual penetration, replacing the gender-specific crime of rape with a series of gender-neutral offenses categorized by the absence or presence of aggravating circumstances.
> ❑ The consent standard was changed so that the victim is not required to physically resist the attacker, and the requirement that the victim's testimony be corroborated was abolished. These changes recognize that submission can be obtained by methods other than overt force.
> ❑ The use of a victim's prior sexual conduct as evidence is now limited. Rape shield laws have been enacted in every state except Utah. Rape shield laws restrict how much victims can be asked about their sexual history.[36]
> ❑ As of 1985, 14 states had enacted statutes making the rape of a woman by her spouse a crime.[37]
> ❑ OVC and the Criminal Justice Section of the American Bar Association (ABA) collaborated on a model statute granting the privilege of confidentiality to rape victim counselors.[38]
> ❑ In 1992, Congress passed the Campus Crime Sexual Assault Bill of Rights, which ensures that campus authorities treat sexual assault victims with dignity and respect, inform victims of their legal rights and options, and cooperate with victims in the exercise of those rights.[39]

In addition to statutorial changes, the various components of the criminal justice system have instituted changes to improve their handling of sexual assault cases. Police departments have created sex crime units to improve their responses to rape. They have also developed inhouse victim/witness assistance units that review reports, contact victims, make referrals to rape crisis centers, and provide community education in rape awareness and prevention. Prosecutors have developed specialized units, which include investigators and victim advocates, to streamline the prosecutorial process. Judges have been provided with the training and

---

[36] Spohn, Cassia and Julie Horney. 1992. *Rape Law Reform: A Grassroots Revolution and Its Impact.* New York: Plenum Press.
[37] Finkelhor, David and Kersti Yllo. 1985. *License to Rape.* New York, NY: Holt, Rinehart, and Winston.
[38] Office for Victims of Crime. 1986. "Privileged communication between victim and counselor: A model statute." *Response* 9(3):13. Washington, DC: U.S. Department of Justice.
[39] Campus Sexual Assault Bill of Rights of 1992, H.R. 2363.

resources necessary to handle rape cases in a sensitive manner. In addition, curriculums have been developed to inform judges of the special needs of rape victims.

Approximately 2,000 organizations have been established to provide services and support to victims of rape.[40] The list includes OVC, which provides grants to states for programs with direct services for all victims of crime, including rape crisis centers and victim compensation centers.[41]

Stalking

Stalking gained national attention because of the 1989 murder of actress Rebecca Schaeffer and reports of a fan's persistent harassment of comedian David Letterman. Although it was the celebrity of these victims that catapulted the problem of stalking to the forefront, most stalking victims are ordinary women who are attempting to end a relationship with a man, often one who has been abusive. Some domestic violence advocates contend that up to 80 percent of stalking incidents occur in a domestic context.[42]

California was the first state to address the problem of stalking by enacting an antistalking statute in 1990. California's law was enacted in response to the murder of five women, including Rebecca Schaeffer, who had been stalking victims. By 1995, 49 states and the District of Columbia had enacted legislation prohibiting stalking. Maine is the only state without a specific law to address stalking; however, it uses a terrorizing statute to combat stalking, and the state's protective order statute was augmented in 1993 to allow orders to be issued to prohibit stalking.[43] Although no common definition across states for stalking exists, most state statutes define stalking as willful, malicious, and repeated following and harassing of another person.[44] Many states require that the stalker exhibit a pattern of conduct and an intent to instill fear in the victim.

Federal involvement in the problem of stalking became prominent in 1993 when Congress directed NIJ to develop a model antistalking code. The intent was to encourage states to implement antistalking legislation and to

---

[40] Office for Victims of Crime. 1996. *Victim of Justice: A New Day Dawns*. Resource Guide. Washington, DC: U.S. Department of Justice.
[41] Victims of Crime Act of 1984.
[42] See, for example, Cheyl Tyiska, National Organization for Victim Assistance. As cited in Lewin, T. "New laws address old problem: The terror of a stalker's threats," *New York Times* 8 February 1993, p. A1.
[43] Bureau of Justice Assistance. 1995. *Regional Seminar Series on Implementing Antistalking Codes*. Monograph. Washington, DC: U.S. Department of Justice.
[44] Ibid., p. 13.

provide direction in formulating these laws.[45] BJA and OVC were also instrumental in these legislative efforts by funding regional seminars, which acquainted state policymakers with the model antistalking code.[46]

Juvenile Victimization

Much of the victimization that women experience begins during childhood and continues throughout their lives. Statistics pertaining to violent offenses committed against juveniles illustrate the alarming frequency with which young people are victimized in this country each year. For example, in 1992 approximately 1.55 million crimes were committed against juveniles between the ages 12 and 17. This represents an increase of 23.4 percent over the 1.26 million figure for 1987.[47] Moreover, nearly one in four violent crimes in 1992 involved a juvenile victim.[48]

The figures for specific offenses, such as child maltreatment, provide further evidence that young people are at considerable risk for victimization (see exhibit 3–5). These statistics demonstrate the need for sexual abuse prevention education for younger children, adolescents, and young adults. In addition, it is important to educate parents about developing safety plans, detecting early signs of child sexual abuse, and listening to and acting on behalf of children.

Elderly Victimization

Adults age 65 and older are less likely than other age groups to experience criminal victimization. When they are victimized, however, their injuries tend to be more serious, affecting their independence and often resulting in an increased fear of crime. Elderly victims of violent crime are more likely to be victimized at or near their homes than victims under the age of 65. Low-income elderly persons are more likely to experience a

---

[45] U.S. Departments of Commerce, Justice, and State, and the Judiciary and Related Agencies Appropriations Act for Fiscal Year 1993, Pub. L. No. 102:395, 106 Arr. 1842.
[46] Bureau of Justice Assistance. 1995. *Regional Seminar Series on Implementing Antistalking Codes.* Monograph. Washington, DC: U.S. Department of Justice.
[47] Moone, Joseph. 1994. *Juvenile Victimizations: 1987 to 1992.* Fact Sheet. Washington, DC: Office of Juvenile Justice and Delinquency Prevention.
[48] Ibid.

violent crime but are less likely to experience theft than elderly persons with high incomes.[49]

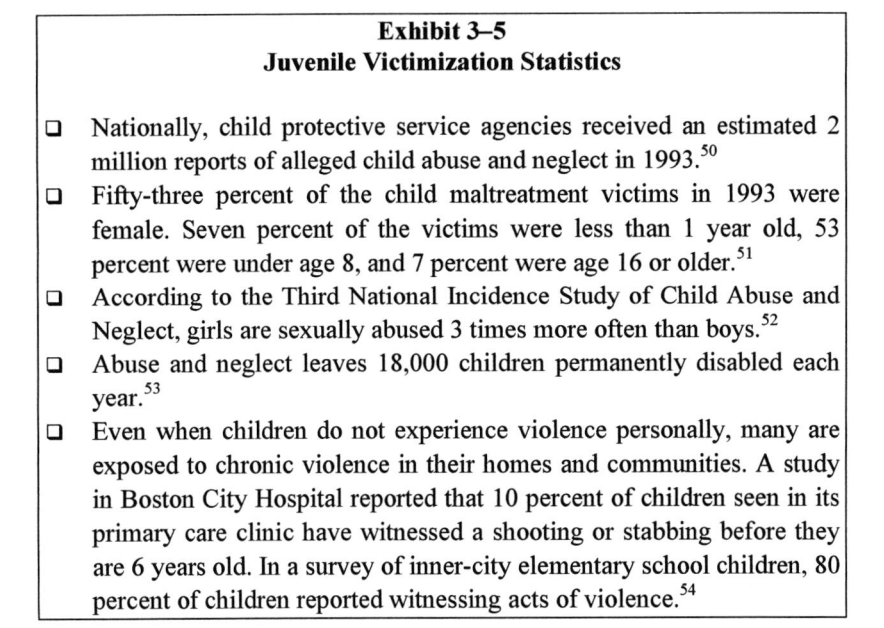

Exhibit 3–5
Juvenile Victimization Statistics

- Nationally, child protective service agencies received an estimated 2 million reports of alleged child abuse and neglect in 1993.[50]
- Fifty-three percent of the child maltreatment victims in 1993 were female. Seven percent of the victims were less than 1 year old, 53 percent were under age 8, and 7 percent were age 16 or older.[51]
- According to the Third National Incidence Study of Child Abuse and Neglect, girls are sexually abused 3 times more often than boys.[52]
- Abuse and neglect leaves 18,000 children permanently disabled each year.[53]
- Even when children do not experience violence personally, many are exposed to chronic violence in their homes and communities. A study in Boston City Hospital reported that 10 percent of children seen in its primary care clinic have witnessed a shooting or stabbing before they are 6 years old. In a survey of inner-city elementary school children, 80 percent of children reported witnessing acts of violence.[54]

A report from the House Select Committee on Aging found that between 1 and 2 million seniors experience elder abuse each year.[55] Yet elderly persons are less likely to report elder or spouse abuse than other crimes committed against them.[56] Neglect is the most common form of elder maltreatment in domestic settings. Forty-five percent of the reports of abuse substantiated in 1991 that did not involve self-neglect involved neglect by a

---

[49] Bachman, Ronet. 1992. *Elderly Victims*. Special Report. Washington, DC: U.S. Department of Justice.
[50] Snyder, Howard N., Melissa Sickmund, and Eileen Poe-Yamagata. *Juvenile Offenders and Victims: 1996 Update on Violence.*
[51] Ibid.
[52] Sedlak, Andrea J., and Diane D. Broadhurst. 1996. *Executive Summary of the Third National Incidence Study of Child Abuse and Neglect*. Washington, DC: U.S. Department of Health and Human Services.
[53] U.S. Advisory Board on Child Abuse and Neglect. 1995. *A Nation's Shame: Child Abuse and Neglect in the United States.* Washington, DC.
[54] Thornberry, Terence P. 1994. *Violent Families and Youth Violence*. Fact Sheet #21. Washington, DC: Office of Juvenile Justice and Delinquency Prevention.
[55] U.S. Congress, House Select Committee on Aging, Subcommittee on Human Services. *Elder Abuse: What Can Be Done?* 102nd Congress, 1st Session, 1991. Washington, DC.
[56] Bachman, Ronet. *Elderly Victims.*

caregiver.[57] The most frequent abusers of the elderly in domestic settings are adult children; almost 33 percent of the substantiated cases of elder abuse in 1991 involved adult children as abusers.[58] The majority of elder abusers were male (51.8 percent in 1991), and approximately two-thirds of victims were females (67.8 percent in 1991).[59]

Cycle of Violence

The cycle of violence begins when children who are raised in abusive homes use drugs and alcohol at an early age to mask the pain. The children leave the home, often become involved in criminal activity to support their habit, and often have children of their own at a very young age. These young parents frequently abuse their children as they were abused and continue their criminal activity because they do not have an education or job skills with which to support themselves and their children. As they are arrested, convicted, and often incarcerated, the family falls apart. Their children are placed with family or in foster care, and are then at risk themselves.

Being abused or neglected in childhood may not only have adverse impacts on an individual's emotional and mental development, but may also increase the likelihood that an individual will engage in criminal or abusive behavior as an adult. According to research by Cathy Spatz Widom, African-American and Caucasian children who are abused and neglected are more likely than nonabused children to be arrested.[60] Abused African-American children are more likely than Caucasians to show an increased likelihood of arrest for violent crimes. Widom suggests that the findings for African-Americans may be due to poverty, family factors, characteristics of the abuse/neglect, lack of access to counseling or support services, and treatment by juvenile authorities.

In subsequent work on the cycle of violence, Widom's preliminary findings substantiate her earlier work.[61] Nearly half of the victims in the initial study had been arrested for some type of nontraffic offense. Eighteen percent of the victims had been arrested for a violent offense, which

---

[57] Tatara, Toshio. 1993. *Summaries of the Statistical Data on Elder Abuse in Domestic Settings for Fiscal Year 1990 and Fiscal Year 1991*. Washington, DC: National Aging Resource Center on Elder Abuse.
[58] Ibid.
[59] Ibid.
[60] Widom, Cathy Spatz. 1992. *The Cycle of Violence*. Research in Brief. Washington, DC: National Institute of Justice.
[61] Widom, Cathy Spatz. 1996. *The Cycle of Violence Revisited*. Research Preview. Washington, DC: National Institute of Justice.

represents a 6-percent increase in the 6 years since arrest records were first checked. Rates of arrest for violent offenses among neglected children were almost as high as rates for physically abused children. Moreover, Widom found that abuse and neglect had a considerable impact on females. Other findings on this topic include the following:

- The likelihood of arrest was 77 percent higher for females who were abused or neglected in childhood than for comparison group females.[62]

- Females who had been abused were significantly more likely than nonabused control females to engage in prostitution. More than 9 percent of abused/neglected females, compared with 2.6 percent of the control females, reported having engaged in prostitution.[63]

- The type of abuse females experienced influenced the rate at which they engaged in prostitution. Physically abused females had the highest rates (13 percent) followed by sexually abused (11.4 percent) and neglected females (9.2 percent).[64]

- Abused/neglected females were at an increased risk for alcoholism. Moreover, abused and/or neglected females were significantly more likely to have alcohol or drug arrests in adulthood than control females.

The research by Widom on the cycle of violence is further supported by the *Survey of State Prison Inmates, 1991.*[65] Results from the survey indicate that 31 percent of females in state prisons reported that they had been abused before age 18, and 24 percent after age 18. These women were equally likely to report either sexual or physical abuse prior to entering prison. Furthermore, females were more likely than male inmates to report having been abused in the past (43 percent versus 12 percent respectively).[66]

---

[62] Widom, Cathy Spatz. *The Cycle of Violence.*
[63] Widom, Cathy Spatz, and Joseph B. Kuhns. Forthcoming. *Childhood Victimization and Subsequent Risk for Promiscuity, Prostitution, and Teenage Pregnancy.*
[64] Ibid.
[65] Beck, Allen et al. 1993. *Survey of State Prison Inmates, 1991.* Washington, DC: Bureau of Justice Statistics.
[66] Snell, Tracy L. 1994. *Women in Prison.* Special Report. Washington, DC: U.S. Department of Justice.

National Response to Violence against Women

Public pressure for a national response to the considerable violence perpetrated against women prompted Congress to pass the Violence Against Women Act as a part of the Violent Crime Control and Law Enforcement Act of 1994.[67] The four subtitles within VAWA—Safe Streets for Women Act, Safe Homes for Women, Civil Rights for Women, and Protection for Battered Immigrant Women and Children—address domestic violence, stalking, and sexual assault, and provide protection against crime motivated by gender. In addition, VAWA responds to the need for fundamental changes in addressing violence against women (see exhibit 3–6).

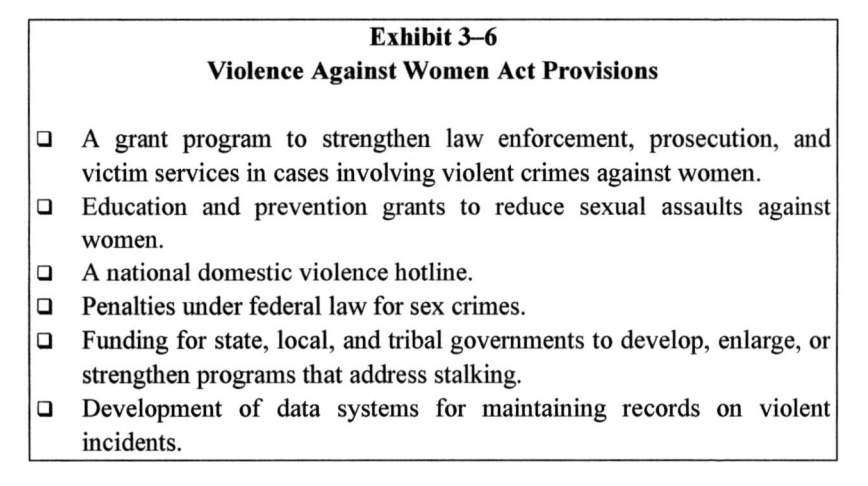

Exhibit 3–6
Violence Against Women Act Provisions

- A grant program to strengthen law enforcement, prosecution, and victim services in cases involving violent crimes against women.
- Education and prevention grants to reduce sexual assaults against women.
- A national domestic violence hotline.
- Penalties under federal law for sex crimes.
- Funding for state, local, and tribal governments to develop, enlarge, or strengthen programs that address stalking.
- Development of data systems for maintaining records on violent incidents.

ADULT FEMALE OFFENDERS AS VICTIMS

Little information is available regarding the victimization of female offenders. One primary source of information comes from a survey of state prison inmates sponsored by the Bureau of Justice Statistics (BJS). The most recent survey, conducted in 1991, included a series of questions about any abuse experienced prior to incarceration and the age at the time of the incident(s). For the first time in a BJS inmate survey, respondents were asked to identify their relationships to their abusers and to indicate whether any sexual abuse involved rape.

---

[67] Violent Crime Control and Law Enforcement Act of 1994.

An estimated 43 percent of women in state prisons in 1991 reported they had been abused, either physically or sexually, prior to their current incarceration. More than three-quarters of these inmates reported being sexually abused. Among the victims of sexual abuse, 56 percent of the abused women said that their abuse had involved a rape, and 13 percent reported an attempted rape. Of the women reporting some prior abuse, half named an intimate as their abuser and more than half (56 percent) named a relative.[68]

Approximately one-third of the women in prison in 1991 were serving a sentence for a violent offense. Almost 67 percent of these women had victimized a relative, an intimate, or an acquaintance. A prior abusive relationship was found to correlate with the criminal behavior of these women; those reporting a history of abuse were more likely to be serving a sentence for a violent offense (42 percent) than were women who did not report being abused (25 percent). A history of prior abuse also affected the type of violent offense committed; 50 percent of the violent female inmates with a history of abuse were serving a sentence for homicide. In comparison, 40 percent of the violent female inmates without a history of abuse were serving a sentence for homicide.[69]

STAFF VICTIMIZATION

People who work in the criminal justice system, especially those in law enforcement and corrections, face unique employment challenges. These challenges are enhanced by the nature of the setting and the constant contact with offenders. The potential for conflict and subsequent staff victimization is an ever-present issue. No information was available on the victimization of criminal justice employees in 1975. Unfortunately, although a few efforts have been launched to address the problem, there is still a lack of data on the overall incidence of these types of offenses.

Between 1991 and 1994, OVC funded the Crime Victims and Corrections project, which trained officials in 12 states on a variety of victim-related areas, including staff victimization.[70] In a survey conducted as part of the project, the National Victim Center (NVC) found that only 32

---

[68] Ibid.
[69] Ibid.
[70] National Victim Center. 1992. *Crime Victims and Corrections: Implementing the Agenda for the 1990's.* Training and Technical Assistance Project Report. Washington, DC: Office for Victims of Crime, U.S. Department of Justice.

adult correctional agencies, 27 juvenile correctional agencies, and 16 parole agencies had written policies on how to handle critical incidents in which personnel became victims or witnesses.[71] In 1996, OVC renewed funding for this project, providing funding to train officials in four additional states and expanding the scope of training to include jail personnel. The material generated by the project could easily be developed into a technical assistance document for all correctional agencies.

The extent of on-the-job victimization is not known since no one is charged with collecting this information nationwide. The 1991 Victims and Corrections Survey revealed that the results of disciplinary hearings for inmates are often not known to the assaulted staff member since most hearings are internal and frequently the inmate is moved to another institution or living unit. In other situations, nothing is done, and the staff member is forced to continue to work in that unit. The way staff are treated by their coworkers, supervisors, and management after a victimization has an enormous impact on how the injured person will perform his or her job and might ultimately affect his or her career in correctional or criminal justice work.

Although it is difficult to accurately measure the extent of job-related staff victimizations, the Federal Government *does* collect some information on federal officers as shown in exhibit 3–7.

Exhibit 3–7
Assaults on Federal Officers, 1979 and 1995

Agency	1979	1995
U.S. Department of Justice	208	299
Bureau of Prisons	99	a
Drug Enforcement Administration	2	65
Federal Bureau of Investigation	43	40
Immigration and Naturalization Service	41	180
U.S. and Assistant U.S. Attorney	4	a
U.S. Marshals Service	19	14

[a] Beginning in 1991, assault statistics from BOP, U.S. and Assistant U.S. Attorneys, and the judicial branch were no longer collected.
Source: Bureau of Justice Statistics. *Sourcebook of Criminal Justice Statistics, 1996,* p. 352. Washington, DC: U.S. Department of Justice.

---

[71] National Victim Center. 1991. *National Victim Services Survey of Adult and Juvenile Corrections and Parole Agencies.* Washington, DC: Office for Victims of Crime, U.S. Department of Justice.

CONCLUSION

There have been significant changes made in the criminal justice system's response to female victims of crime since 1975. Changes such as the criminalization of domestic violence and the establishment of sexual assault treatment centers demonstrate the recognition of the serious nature of such crimes and the need for appropriate interventions. The progress made in response to female victims of crime is primarily attributed to the efforts of the crime victims movement, often championed by women. At the forefront, women have been working to enact crime victims bills of rights, constitutional amendments, and other enabling statutes to serve all crime victims. One significant aspect of these efforts was the passage of the Violence Against Women Act in 1994, which affords women greater safety and provides protection against crimes motivated by gender.

Despite these changes, current data on violence against women illustrate the need for additional measures such as a coordinated and integrated approach to reduce and prevent victimization of women. A coordinated approach to this problem suggests collaboration among law enforcement, prosecution offices, and the courts, as well as victim advocates and service providers. For the criminal justice system's response to be effective, professionals within the system should share a vision that prioritizes the safety and well-being of female victims.

RECOMMENDATIONS FROM THE OJP COORDINATION GROUP ON WOMEN

1. Develop new correctional agency policies using examples of promising practices to enhance victim services.
2. Develop more training curriculums for crime victim services personnel.
3. Develop offender programming and services that address the offender's past victimization and its impact on his or her criminal behavior.
4. Expand juvenile victimization prevention programs.
5. Provide information to criminal justice agencies regarding state or federal programs and services that assist staff and offenders who have been victimized or who witness victimization.

6. Fund research and evaluation of the effectiveness of victim-awareness initiatives, such as Impact of Crime on Victims courses.
7. Develop techniques to collect data on crimes committed against victims under the age of 12.
8. Fund research to assess the effectiveness of victim notification systems.
9. Fund research to identify and evaluate treatment approaches for female victims of abuse.
10. Fund research to collect data on the victimization of females working in the criminal justice system and the work-related impact of those incidents.
11. Continue funding for research on the viability of restorative justice approaches that influence intervention for cases involving violence against women.

Chapter 4

WOMEN WHO WORK IN THE CRIMINAL JUSTICE SYSTEM

INTRODUCTION

With regard to women who work in the criminal justice system, *The Report of the LEAA* [Law Enforcement Assistance Administration] *Task Force on Women* (hereafter referred to as the 1975 report) focused solely on women employed in the former LEAA [currently the Office of Justice Programs (OJP)]. This chapter takes a different perspective, looking at women working in the criminal justice and juvenile justice systems, such as wardens, attorneys, judges, and police.[*]

Title VII of the Civil Rights Act of 1964 amended the foundation for occupational opportunities for women. Notwithstanding some gains in the upper ranks of a male-dominated field, improvement is still needed. Issues discussed in this chapter include barriers to recruitment, retention, and advancement of women in the criminal justice system related to gender bias; the "glass ceiling"; sexual harassment; and training and technical assistance opportunities. Since 1975, the number of women working in the criminal justice system has dramatically increased (see exhibit 4-1 for recent figures). Specific areas discussed in this chapter include:

---

[*] It is important to note that today women occupy several key positions in the U.S. Department of Justice (DOJ) as U.S. Attorney General, U.S. Assistant Attorney General for the Office of Justice Programs, Director of the Federal Bureau of Prisons, and the Director of the Immigration and Naturalization Service.

- ❑ Women working in law enforcement.
- ❑ Women working in the courts.
- ❑ Women working in adult corrections.
- ❑ Women working in juvenile corrections.
- ❑ Gender bias through the glass ceiling and organizational culture.
- ❑ Sexual harassment.
- ❑ Training.

Exhibit 4-1
Women Who Work in the Criminal Justice System, 1995

- ❑ Women constitute nearly 30 percent of all correctional personnel in state adult correctional facilities and 35 percent of all correctional personnel in juvenile systems.[1,2]
- ❑ Seventeen percent of the wardens or superintendents in state correctional systems and 20 percent in juvenile systems are female.[3]
- ❑ Thirty percent of all jail payroll staff and 24 percent of all jail correctional officers are female.[4]
- ❑ Women hold 12 percent of the supervisory and 11 percent of the nonsupervisory correctional officer positions in the federal adult correctional system.[5]

WOMEN WORKING IN LAW ENFORCEMENT

Although women have been involved in police work in the United States for more than 80 years, their concerns regarding participation in law enforcement and career advancement have remained constant for nearly 60 of those years. Not until the 1960s, when legislation and judicial involvement began to support women's demands for equality, did their duties and responsibilities begin to expand (see exhibit 4-2). Since then,

---

[1] Stephan, James J. 1997. *Census of State and Federal Correctional Facilities, 1995*, p. 18. Washington, DC: U.S. Department of Justice.
[2] Bureau of Justice Statistics. 1996. *Sourcebook of Criminal Justice Statistics, 1995*, p. 103. Washington, DC: U.S. Department of Justice.
[3] Bureau of Justice Statistics. 1997. *Sourcebook of Criminal Justice Statistics, 1996*, p. 89. Washington, DC: U.S. Department of Justice.
[4] Perkins, Craig A., James J. Stephan, and Allen J. Beck. 1995. *Jails and Jail Inmates, 1993-94*. Bureau of Justice Statistics Bulletin, p. 8. Washington, DC: U.S. Department of Justice.
[5] Bureau of Justice Statistics. 1995. *Sourcebook of Criminal Justice Statistics, 1994*, pp. 94-95. Washington, DC: U.S. Department of Justice.

opportunities for women in policing have improved, but female police officers continue to make slow progress through the ranks.

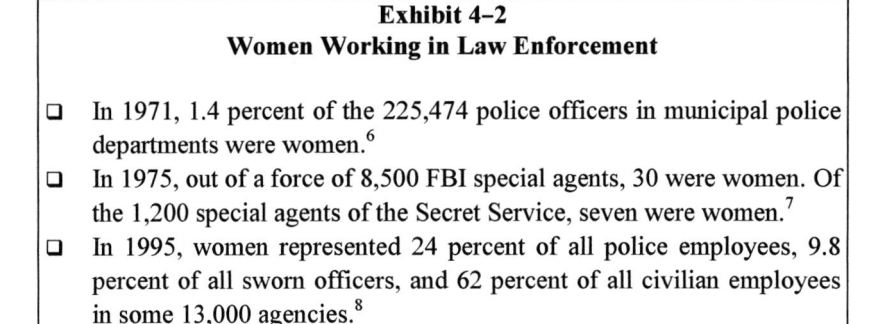

Exhibit 4-2
Women Working in Law Enforcement

❑ In 1971, 1.4 percent of the 225,474 police officers in municipal police departments were women.[6]
❑ In 1975, out of a force of 8,500 FBI special agents, 30 were women. Of the 1,200 special agents of the Secret Service, seven were women.[7]
❑ In 1995, women represented 24 percent of all police employees, 9.8 percent of all sworn officers, and 62 percent of all civilian employees in some 13,000 agencies.[8]

Gender inequity is deeply ingrained in the workplace and is based on societal expectations and attitudes. An analysis of gender inequity in the workplace, with emphasis on the employment of women in jails, determined that women face major obstacles in male-dominated areas such as law enforcement and corrections and find it difficult to become managers.[9] Women are denied training, lack agency-sponsored opportunities for networking, and are limited by traditional organizational behavior in these fields.

In a 1991 article, S. E. Martin indicates that, although both court-ordered and voluntary affirmative action policies have had a significant impact on the hiring of female officers, they have not affected the promotion and advancement of women into the higher ranks of law enforcement agencies.[10] The progress made by women in policing has come primarily through legal mandates rather than executive leadership within organizations.[11] According to Amy Ramson's 1993 report for the Police Foundation, no systematic discrimination was found with respect to the

---

[6] House, Cathryn H. 1993. "The changing role of women in law enforcement." *Police Chief* 60(10): 142.
[7] Ibid.
[8] Uniform Crime Reporting Division of the Federal Bureau of Investigation. 1996. *Crime in the United States, 1995*, p. 283. Washington, DC: U.S. Department of Justice.
[9] Cornish, A.R. 1994. "Impact of the 'Glass Ceiling' on women employed in Florida jails." In *Human Resources in Criminal Justice*, eds. D.L. Zahm, C. Stiff, et al. Tallahassee, FL: Department of Law Enforcement.
[10] Martin, S.E. 1991. "Effectiveness of affirmative action: The case of women in policing." *Justice Quarterly* 8(4): 489-504.
[11] McCoy, D.G. 1993. "Women in law enforcement: A positive work environment." *Law Enforcement Tomorrow* 2(1): 5-9.

recruitment of women into policing.[12] Ramson added, however, that the number of female applicants and recruits remains low, a point underscored by Phyllis MacDonald, a former policewoman and current social science analyst with the National Institute of Justice (NIJ).[13] With a recruitment rate of only 20 percent, it is unlikely that the percentage of women in policing will increase significantly.

Despite advances in supervisory positions, female police chiefs remain exceptions. According to a 1996 interview with Police Chief Carol Mehrling (Montgomery County, Maryland), "Our biggest barriers are often ourselves . . . [You must] realize that you may be ahead of your time and keep moving forward—belief in yourself may be the first impression a person or supervisor sees, [so] make every contact positive and genuine."[14]

Some studies have cited specific problems and coping strategies. In a 1992 article, Harry W. More concludes that the primary obstacle women must overcome concerns male officers' attitudes.[15] More's conclusions are supported by the 1992 findings of Donna C. Hale, who found that the attitudes of male officers and supervisors have been the main obstacle faced by women and can be addressed through specific measures designed to accomplish complete integration of law enforcement agencies.[16] M.C. Brown published the results of a 1994 survey suggesting that policing would benefit from more research regarding gender-related attitudes, active recruitment of women, and the establishment of an all-woman council to review complaints of female police officers.[17]

In 1992, D.G. McCoy examined organizational structures that would support a positive work environment for women.[18] McCoy recommended the development and implementation of policies and practices to create an organizational culture that uses the distinctive qualities of policewomen, thereby enabling them to take advantage of the same career opportunities as male officers. This environment would value the complex role and competing interests that women face in both society and the workplace. The study concluded that most police executives in 1992 had not created

---

[12] Ramson, Amy. 1993. "Women in policing: A success story." *Womenpolice* 27(4): 15-19.
[13] MacDonald, Phyllis. Interview by Jodi Zepp, February 1996.
[14] Mehrling, Carol. Interview by Jodi Zepp, via correspondence, April 1, 1996.
[15] More, Harry W. 1992. "Male-dominated police culture: Reducing the gender gap." In *Special Topics in Policing*, 113-137. Cincinnati, OH: Anderson Publishing Co.
[16] Hale, Donna C. 1992. "Women in policing." In *What Works in Policing: Operations and Administration Examined*, eds. G.W. Cordner and D.C. Hale. Cincinnati, OH: Anderson Publishing Co.
[17] Brown, M.C. 1994. "Plight of female police: A survey of NW patrolmen." *Police Chief* 61(9): 50-53.
[18] McCoy, D.G. 1993. "Women in law enforcement: A positive work environment."

organizational cultures that valued the diversity of women within law enforcement. McCoy recommended an executive commitment to creating an organizational structure that provides training on the value of diversity in the workforce and demonstrates agency support for women by providing mentoring for career development.[19]

WOMEN WORKING IN THE COURTS

Female professionals in the court systems have experienced considerable advancements since 1975 (see exhibit 4-3). Nevertheless, today gender bias is still often evident. Forty states and nine federal circuits appointed task forces to investigate the extent of gender bias in their jurisdictions. In several of these reports, it was noted that in court, female lawyers may be called *honey, little lady,* and *little girl* or be referred to by their first names when their male colleagues are referred to as "Mr. _____."[20] According to the American Bar Association's *Report on the Status of Women in the Legal Profession,* sexual bias in the courtroom may affect not only the interpersonal relationship between the judge and the female attorney, but also the outcome of a case.[21] If a female attorney takes an aggressive posture in litigation, a judge may interpret her behavior as unnecessary drama; if a woman appears to be too cool in court, she may be perceived as being unsupportive of her client.[22] Minority female lawyers have the additional burden of being mistaken for clients when they appear in court.[23]

---

[19] McCoy, D.G. 1992. *Future Organizational Environment for Women in Law Enforcement.* Sacramento, CA: California Commission on Peace Officer Standards and Training.

[20] Bernat, Francis P. 1992. "Women in the legal profession." In *The Changing Roles of Women in the Criminal Justice System,* ed. Imogene L. Moyer. Prospect Heights, IL: Waveland Press.

[21] Commission on Women in the Profession. *Report on the Status of Women in the Legal Profession.* American Bar Association.

[22] As cited in Bernat, Francis P. "Women in the legal profession."

[23] Ibid.

> **Exhibit 4–3**
> **Women Working in the Courts**
>
> ❑ About 80 percent of female lawyers have entered the profession since 1970.[24]
> ❑ About 44 percent of all first-year law students are women; as of 1995, women accounted for roughly 23 percent of all attorneys—a 13-percent increase since 1985.[25]
> ❑ Twenty percent of solo practitioners are women, and 39 percent of law firms employ female attorneys.[26]
> ❑ Women represent 28 percent of all government lawyers, 38 percent of all legal aid and public defender program lawyers, and 28 percent of all professionals employed in legal education.[27]
> ❑ From 1980 to 1991, representation of women among state judges increased from 4 to 9 percent; women represented 12 percent of intermediate appellate court judges, 10 percent of trial court judges, and 9.5 percent of all courts-of-last-resort judges.[28]
> ❑ As of 1996 there were 146 sitting female federal judges, 17 percent of whom were active judges and 2 percent of whom were senior judges. Between 1975 and 1995, 159 females were appointed to the bench. President Carter appointed 42 women, President Reagan appointed 32 women, President Bush appointed 37 women, and President Clinton appointed 48 women to the bench in that time period.[29]

Female lawyers and judges are often assigned to represent or decide cases in areas traditionally considered the purview of women—family and civil matters. Typically, cases in these areas have lower status and fewer contacts for persons seeking political careers than cases in other areas.

---

[24] Commission on Women in the Profession. December 1995. "Basic facts from women in the law: A look at the numbers." In *Unfinished Business*. American Bar Association.
[25] Ibid.
[26] Ibid.
[27] Ibid.
[28] Ibid.
[29] Federal Judicial History Office, Federal Judicial Center. 1996. Unpublished data. Washington, DC.

WOMEN WORKING IN ADULT CORRECTIONS

Although there have been gains in female employment, corrections remains the most sex-segregated and male-dominated component of the criminal justice system (see exhibit 4-4).[30] Issues of security, inmate privacy, and physical qualifications have been cited in the past as outweighing women's rights to equal opportunity. These barriers have largely been removed, although subtler barriers remain.

According to a 1984 study by R. Etheridge, being hired and assigned to a post is only the beginning. The most important elements that a woman can bring to a job is confidence that she can do the job and a realistic approach to deal with and learn from difficulties.[31] A woman faces overprotection as well as unfair competition. Etheridge found that supervisors' behavior also can be affected by perceptions of a female employee as daughter or wife because those are the female roles they understand.[32]

Exhibit 4-4
Women Working in Adult Corrections

- Women hold 12 percent of the supervisory and 12 percent of the nonsupervisory correctional officer positions in the federal adult system.[33]
- Women make up nearly 30 percent of all correctional personnel in state adult correctional facilities.[34]
- Seventeen percent of women in state adult correctional systems are wardens or superintendents.[35]
- Some female wardens have moved to other upper management positions; 6.9 percent of all federal wardens are female.[36]

---

[30] Feinman, Clarice. 1994. *Women in the Criminal Justice System*, pp. 159, 165. Westport, CT: Praeger Publishers.
[31] Etheridge, R., et al. 1984. "Female employees in all-male correctional facilities." *Federal Probation* 48(4): 54–65.
[32] Ibid.
[33] Bureau of Justice Statistics. 1995. *Sourcebook of Criminal Justice Statistics, 1994*, pp. 94–95.
[34] Stephan, James J. *Census of State and Federal Correctional Facilities, 1995*, p. 18.
[35] Bureau of Justice Statistics. *Sourcebook of Criminal Justice Statistics, 1996*, p. 89.
[36] Bureau of Justice Statistics. *Sourcebook of Criminal Justice Statistics, 1994*, p. 96.

WOMEN WORKING IN JUVENILE CORRECTIONS

In a survey of juvenile corrections agencies, Marjorie H. Young examined factors contributing to the successful promotion of women to leadership positions and identified barriers women have encountered while working in these traditionally male-dominated positions (see exhibit 4–5). Factors that the respondents said led to their success included concern for children, a vision for change, an ability to work well with men, and experience in juvenile corrections. Many respondents said that they felt that their employers did not perceive them as working on a career track, that their male colleagues did not take them seriously, and that they constantly had to prove their abilities. Young's findings show that there is a need to address the pressures women face in combining job and family demands, achieving leadership positions, and being accepted as supervisors and managers of men.[37]

Exhibit 4–5
Women Working in Juvenile Corrections

- Women constitute 35 percent of all correctional personnel in state juvenile correctional facilities.[38]
- Nearly 20 percent of women in state juvenile correctional systems hold the position of warden or superintendent.[39]

GENDER BIAS: THE GLASS CEILING AND ORGANIZATIONAL CULTURE

The 1975 report noted a concern for a prevailing, outmoded attitude toward women in the work environment. Myths and stereotypes about women were among the obstacles examined by the report. The continued presence of these obstacles is evident by the relatively small numbers of women gaining employment in the criminal justice system and their difficulty in achieving promotions and leadership positions. In various criminal justice agencies, some levels of employment remain beyond the

---

[37] Young, Marjorie H. 1992. "Examining keys to success for today's women working in juvenile corrections." *Corrections Today* 54(6): 106–111.
[38] Bureau of Justice Statistics. *Sourcebook of Criminal Justice Statistics, 1994*, p. 93.
[39] Bureau of Justice Statistics. *Sourcebook of Criminal Justice Statistics, 1996*, p.89.

reach of women and minorities despite the apparent gains women have made in the workforce since 1975. This barrier is known as the glass ceiling.

In the 1991 *A Report on the Glass Ceiling Initiative*, the U.S. Department of Labor found that attitudinal and organizational barriers are an indication that the progress of minorities and women in corporate America is affected by more than qualifications and career choices.[40]

Several general findings applied to the companies in the study included:

- There is a point beyond which minorities and women have not advanced in some companies. Minorities have plateaued at lower levels of the workforce than women.

- Monitoring for equal access and opportunity, especially as managers move up the corporate ladder to senior management, was almost never considered corporate responsibility nor part of the planning for developmental programs and policies.

- Appraisal and total compensation systems that determine salary, bonuses, incentives, and prequisites for employees were not monitored.

Among the attitudinal and organizational barriers identified were:

- Developmental practices and credential-building experiences, including advanced education, and career-enhancing assignments (such as placement on corporate committees and task forces, traditional precursors to advancement) were often not readily available to minorities and women.

- Accountability for Equal Employment Opportunity (EEO) responsibilities did not reach senior executives and corporate decisionmakers.

In 1995, the National Institute of Corrections (NIC) conducted an organizational culture survey of all state directors of corrections and directors of large city jails. Findings suggested that gender inequality is real, although men and women perceive the inequality differently. Women

---

[40] U.S. Department of Labor. 1991. *A Report on the Glass Ceiling Initiative.*

believe that to advance to positions of leadership, they have to work harder and take greater risks than men.[41]

Corrections has had to adjust to the growing number of women in the labor pool. In 1991, the American Correctional Association's (ACA's) Women in Corrections Committee surveyed state adult and juvenile corrections agencies' training programs, particularly programs that targeted female employees and that pointed to specific areas of need that had not been met.[42] Thirty-nine agencies were surveyed (19 adult, 16 youth, and 4 combined), and all agencies had formalized training programs. The results showed that:

- Forty-six percent of the agencies offered training to address specific needs of female employees.
- Seventy-six percent required all staff to take courses in sexual harassment awareness.
- Fifty-nine percent offered training to decrease gender and race bias/stereotyping and to increase awareness and understanding of gender differences.

Adult departments of correction that have youth services agencies have taken a more active role in promoting women's training needs. The primary concern, voiced by 36 percent of these agencies, was for training to understand and help eliminate sexual harassment.

Both the federal prison system and the state corrections systems (including maximum-security prisons) have adopted gender-neutral employment policies. In a 1994 study of gender-neutral employment in high-security prisons, R.H. Rison reported that correctional administrators had taken measures to confront gender bias in their managerial practices.[43] States have implemented gender-neutral hiring practices, for reasons ranging from recognition of equal opportunity and requests by female officers to make high-security positions available, to union pressures and court mandates. In instituting gender neutrality in high-security institutions, administrators are encouraged to develop a plan and optimize the timeframe for

---

[41] K-RAN Design, Inc. 1995. *Curriculum Design Summary Report for the National Institute of Corrections Executive Training for Women.* Salem, NH. For more information, contact Andie Moss at NIC, 202-307-1300.

[42] Bergsmann, Ilene. 1991. "ACA Women in Corrections Committee examines female staff training needs." *Corrections Today* 53(7): 106, 108–109.

[43] Rison, R.H. 1994. "Women as high-security officers: Gender-neutral employment in high-security prisons." *Federal Prisons Journal* 3(3): 1–23.

implementation, provide training and communications, prepare for staff resistance, phase female employees into maximum-security posts, and review their organizational structures for job equality.

Two basic reasons for employing women in corrections are the doctrine of fundamental fairness and the need to expand the talent pool of correctional personnel. This was demonstrated by a study of the gradual changes in policies and practices relating to the employment of women in correctional positions in Michigan over a 20-year period. The presence of women has produced a healthy reexamination of long-standing beliefs and practices in the correctional culture.[44]

Findings from a 1996 study conducted by Joseph R. Rowan support the need to reassess policies pertaining to the assignments of female corrections employees.[45] This study was the first to address the safety of female officers working in maximum security prisons. The data revealed that female correctional officers were less likely than male officers to be assaulted on the job; men were assaulted 3.6 times more often.

In another 1996 study, Rowan demonstrated that female officers are at least as firm as their male counterparts in managing inmates involved in serious incidents. In states with the highest percentage of female officers in the correctional workforce, there were 47 percent fewer assaults on female officers and 41 percent fewer assaults on male officers.[46] When asked to explain the lower rates in assault, the respondents, primarily male administrators, commented that female officers listen better than men, seldom act "macho," have a calming effect, are less confrontational, and often exercise control without using force. The survey mirrors the results of research on the overall performance of female officers in law enforcement agencies nationwide.[47]

The Rowan study concludes that increasing the number of female employees in correctional settings may lower the risk of assault.

As women move up the employment ranks in criminal justice, future lawsuits may center on promotions. When women are fully integrated into both the training and functions of criminal justice agencies, it is likely to favorably affect incidents of sexual harassment, employment obstacles, and

---

[44] Johnson, P.M. 1992. "Why employ women?" *Corrections Today* 54(6): 162–167.
[45] Rowan, Joseph R. 1996. "Who is safer in male maximum security prisons?" *Corrections Today* 58(2): 186–189.
[46] Rowan, Joseph R. 1996. "Female correctional officers said to reduce prison violence." In *Criminal Justice Newsletter,* April, 27(7): 2–3.
[47] Ibid.

other barriers women face. The increasing presence of women in criminal justice agencies has helped broaden the overall perspective of employers.[48]

SEXUAL HARASSMENT

Two types of sexual harassment have been recognized by statutes and the courts. The first is *quid pro quo*, "something for something," and usually applies to situations in which a supervisor or manager has made unwelcome sexual advances, requested sexual favors, or engaged in physical conduct of a sexual nature. The second is "hostile work environment," in which the conduct of another employee, a supervisor, or even a nonemployee may be the basis for the claim. Hostility in the work environment is created by sexual jokes, suggestive comments, suggestive pictures, obscene gestures, unwanted physical contact, and other situations that interfere with an employee's work performance.[49] Different agencies and organizations are making their employees aware of the different types of sexual harassment.

At the organizational level, several jail administrators attending the 1990 National Jails Conference, "Setting the Jail Research Agenda for the 1990s," admitted that they were concerned about the entry of women into traditionally male jobs and the potential "problems" such integration might cause.[50] They were concerned about the potential for sexual harassment in their facilities and their liability for such harassment. According to a 1991 survey that examined the incidence of sexual harassment in local government organizations that provided protective services, women were overrepresented in the group of sexual harassment victims relative to men. Coworkers were the source of most victimizations.[51] A 1988 study by the Federal Office of Policy Evaluation reported similar findings.

The seriousness of this issue is recognized at all levels, including county government. Carol Mehrling, Police Chief of Montgomery County, Maryland, finds that supervisors are the key in creating a tension-free workplace: "Department leaders must make it clear that there is ZERO tolerance. . . . [F]raternization issues must be addressed clearly, starting with academy training, and a swift investigation of complaints will show sincere

---

[48] Martin, D. and M. Levine. 1991. "Status of women in law enforcement." *Law Enforcement Technology* 18(2): 26.
[49] Brown, R., Jr. and M. Van Ochten. 1990. "Sexual harassment: A vulnerable area for corrections." *Corrections Today* 52(5): 62-70.
[50] Beck, Ann C. and Mary K. Stohr. 1991 "Sexual harassment and support for Affirmative Action." *American Jails* 5(5): 15-17.
[51] Ibid.

commitments to the issue."[52] Chief Mehrling notes that some women might misuse this issue for better assignments or retaliation, but the reporting of sexual harassment still remains limited because of fear of reprisals from male coworkers and supervisors.

Some agencies that are responsible for enforcing the laws prohibiting sexual harassment also experience such problems. For example, according to a 1993 *National Law Journal* survey, 73 percent of the responding law firms had a formal written policy for sexual harassment, yet harassment remains a problem.[53] In a 1994 St. Louis Bar Association study, both men and women reported observing at least one incident of sexual harassment by a superior, and more than half of the women surveyed for the 1993 *National Law Journal* study reported having experienced harassment on the job.[54] (Few attorneys—and few women in any part of the criminal justice system—report harassment to firm management.)

Although many approaches to preventing sexual harassment have been suggested, Susan L. Webb, in *Step Forward*, states that those companies and organizations that successfully stop or prevent harassment in their workplaces have comprehensive programs in place that include six elements: (1) top management support; (2) a written, posted policy statement; (3) procedures for receiving and handling complaints; (4) experience in handling complaints; (5) training for all employees; and (6) followthrough.[55]

Even when appropriate programs have been developed, successful implementation requires support from the top. Management's attitude toward sexual harassment may be an obstacle to a program's adoption and effectiveness. In fact, management's attitude—refusing to acknowledge, overlooking, or trivializing the issue—may actually contribute to harassment. Studies have found that the best approaches to success addresses problem solving. A 1988 survey by *Working Woman* magazine reports: "[C]ommitment from the top makes a difference. When senior management is perceived as making the prevention of sexual harassment a top priority, firms are far more likely to offer training programs and to establish mechanisms to encourage the reporting of both formal and informal complaints."

---

[52] Mehrling, Carol. Interview by Jodi Zepp.
[53] American Bar Association Commission on Women in the Profession. "Report on the Status of Women in the Legal Profession."
[54] Ibid.
[55] Webb, Susan. 1991. *Step Forward: Sexual Harassment in the Workplace—What You Need to Know*. USA: Master Media Limited.

TRAINING

Appropriate training will ensure that women are prepared to meet the challenges facing them as employees in the corrections system.[56] Training is necessary to prevent sexual harassment and to ensure that women have the skills required for career advancement. Studies have shown that women are underrepresented in executive-level positions in the corrections field. In response, NIC funded the development of an executive training program to enhance the ability of women to achieve and function effectively in executive positions in state departments of corrections. NIC, along with K-RAN Design, Inc., established an executive training pilot program in September 1994. Participants included female deputy directors or assistant commissioners of corrections in their states. The overall objectives of the training program were to provide executive leadership development for women in corrections, establish strategies for women's long-term promotional success, and facilitate planning that supports personal learning and career opportunities. The executive leadership and training workshops are a continuing element of NIC's curriculum.[57]

NIC also offers an annual seminar, "Management Development for Women and Minorities," specifically targeted to women and minorities who currently or will possibly occupy middle-level administrative positions in corrections. Topics include problem-solving strategies and identification of individual roles, relationships in the workplace, individual strengths and differences, and identification of managerial and leadership styles, skills, and techniques.

ACA offers an annual course entitled "Change, Challenge, and Choices," designed especially for women new to corrections, including case workers, unit managers, and those working in middle management. Topics include mixed-gender employment in corrections, the history of women in corrections, identification of stereotypes, power and conflict management, mentoring and networking, and development of personalized action plans.

In 1987, A. Morrison, R. White, and E. Van Belsor identified a set of factors that proved to be successful for women in corrections. These factors emphasize strategic planning, communications, and decisionmaking.[58] Some

---

[56] Corrothers, Helen G. 1996. "Education and training: The key to enhancement and advancement." In *State of Corrections: Proceedings of the ACA Annual Conferences, 1995*, pp. 133–142. Lanham, MD: American Correctional Association.

[57] K-RAN Design, Inc. 1995. *Curriculum Design Summary Report for the National Institute of Corrections Executive Training for Women.*

[58] Morrison, A., R. White, and E. van Belsor. 1987. "Women with promise: Who succeeds, who fails?" *Career Realities and Strategies*. Salem, NH: K-RAN Designs, Inc.

factors serve as "double-edged swords" in many situations. For example, women must take risks, but must also be consistently outstanding; be tough, but not be macho; be ambitious, but not expect equal treatment; and take responsibility, but also follow others' advice. Put simply, to succeed, female managers and executives must find the overlap between acceptable male and female behaviors that the dominant senior executive male culture finds acceptable.[59] The following represents a list of factors female executives have identified as having been important to their career and promotional success.

- ❑ Help from above—not usually from one person but from several people over time.
- ❑ Consistently outstanding achievement in technical competence, professionalism, leadership, and the ability to spot and head off problems.
- ❑ A commitment to success with a determination to push until the job is done.
- ❑ Superior interpersonal skills and an ability to manage subordinates.
- ❑ Willingness to undertake risks and the challenges necessary to grow professionally and be visible in the workplace.
- ❑ The ability to be tough, decisive, and demanding.

Once women have achieved "success," they must continue the work and training effort to keep their levels of advancement. As Helen G. Corrothers observed:

> Success has been an elusive quality for women in corrections, and the road to its achievement has been rough. . . . [M]any of the qualities and attributes that enabled women to acquire an initial measure of success remain vital to the retention and
>
> advancement or managing of success. The difficulty of the struggle for success places a higher value on its retention.[60]

---

[59] Center for Creative Leadership. 1994. *Career Realities and Strategies*. Salem, NH: K-RAN Designs, Inc.
[60] Corrothers, Helen G. 1991. "Managing success." In *Change, Challenge, and Choices: Women's Role in Modern Corrections*, pp. 67-81. Lanham, MD: American Correctional Association.

CONCLUSION

Significant progress has been made by women employed in the criminal justice field since 1975. This progress has been attributed to such factors as legislation, court decisions, and executive leadership; however, many barriers to the full achievement of women's professional potential still exist. For example, additional career development opportunities should be created in all components of the criminal justice system to handle the challenges of working in male-dominated professions. Mechanisms and initiatives that assist women in career development must be implemented. Financial and familial concerns affect upward mobility and promotional opportunities, as they relate to criminal justice professionals' willingness to relocate. Notwithstanding some progress, the "glass ceiling" remains firmly in place, requiring continued efforts to assist women in career advancement. Finally, efforts that enhance public awareness of the progress made by women must be intensified to encourage their participation in the criminal justice profession.

RECOMMENDATIONS FROM THE OJP COORDINATION GROUP ON WOMEN

1. Develop strategies to enhance job opportunities for women.
2. Continue researching equity issues relative to the recruitment and advancement of women working in criminal justice.
3. Provide staff development and training programs for criminal justice personnel that include assertiveness training, strategic planning, and workplace diversity initiatives. Emphasize the importance of eliminating sexual harassment in the workplace.
4. Highlight women's accomplishments in the criminal justice system through promotional pieces in the media and in professional publications to ensure public awareness of women's many contributions and responsibilities.
5. Implement policies promoting flexibility in criminal justice agencies to enable all employees to balance careers and family life.
6. Discuss gender-sensitive issues at the highest administrative levels to help dispel myths and stereotypes about women.

CONCLUSION

More than 20 years later, female criminal justice professionals continue to search for ways to strengthen agencies' management responses to initiatives within a larger framework with more urgent demands and higher priorities. An example of this can be seen in the corrections system. Many operating correctional agencies still hold that female offenders do not warrant a full management response because they constitute a relatively small percentage of the general population. The system often fails to respond to some of the most obvious difficulties faced by female offenders.

Over the past 20 years, a cross section of professionals have contributed a considerable amount of information to the literature in a number of critical areas such as the impact of welfare reform, girls in adult corrections, the increase of minorities and women in the workforce, the impact of the 1994 Crime Bill, and the establishment of new offices with granting authority. The knowledge gained in each area has led to, among other things, increased comprehension of interactions of the various areas, their interrelationship with one another, and the extent to which they are influenced by forces both within and outside the criminal justice system.

The 1998 Coordination Group on Women will continue its efforts to focus increased attention by the Office of Justice Programs and other U.S. Department of Justice components on the recommendations made in this updated report.

INDEX

A

abuse and exploitation, 31, 35
abuse counseling, xii
adult female offenders, xii, 1, 2
African-American female juveniles, 24
alcohol abuse, 10, 12
American Bar Association (ABA), 56, 71, 72, 79
American Correctional Association (ACA), 12-14, 17, 20, 22, 32, 35, 76, 80, 81

B

Bureau of Justice Assistance (BJA), vii, 5, 53, 57, 58
Bureau of Justice Statistics (BJS), viii, xiii, 2-5, 10, 11, 13-15, 45, 54, 61, 62, 64, 68, 73, 74
Bureau of Prison's (BOP's) Victim Witness Program, 44
Bureau of Prisons (BOP), vii, 13, 17, 18, 44, 64, 67
burglary, 12

C

Campus Crime Sexual Assault Bill of Rights, 56
child abuse prevention and treatment services, 43
classification practices, 8
community programs, xiv, 18
community-based services, xii, 19
correctional agencies, 64, 83
correctional agency policies, xiv, 65
Correctional Education Association (CEA), 13
correctional facilities, 9, 16, 21, 25, 49, 68, 73, 74
correctional system, 4, 68
Crime Victims and Corrections project, 63
criminal justice professionals, xii, 82
criminal justice system, ix, xi, xii, xiii, 2, 3, 6, 8, 9, 13, 20, 27, 31, 37, 45, 47, 50, 51, 53, 54, 56, 63, 65, 66, 67, 73, 74, 82, 83
criminalization of domestic violence, xiii, 65
criminogenic behaviors of female offenders, xiv, 18

D

delinquent activities, 31
delinquent behavior among girls, 30
delinquent behavior, 30, 40
Department of Justice (DOJ), 44, 67
domestic violence programs, 43
domestic violence, xiii, 6, 44, 48, 50, 51-55, 57, 62
drug abuse, 12, 16
drug offenses, xii, 1, 10, 11
drug-related offenses, 1, 2

E

elderly victimization, 50
embezzlement, xii, 1, 2, 10
Equal Employment Opportunity (EEO), 75

F

facility staff, 13
family crises, 16
family-related abuse, 31
Federal Judicial Center, 6, 72
federal prison system, 76
federal prisons, 3, 6, 15
female crime victims, xi, 43, 46
female criminal justice professionals, ix, xi, xii, 83
female drug users, 12
female juvenile crime, ix
female juvenile offender(s), xii, 19-22, 24, 26-35, 37-41
female offenders, xi, 1, 2, 3
female police officers, 69, 70
female victimization, 45
female victims of crime, ix, xiii, 44-47, 65
forgery, xii, 1, 2, 10

G

Gathering Information, Assessing What Works, Interpreting the Facts, Networking with Key Stakeholders, and Stimulating Change (GAINS), 8
gender inequity, 69
gender-neutral employment policies, 76
gender-specific problems, 29
gender-specific programming, xiv, 18
gender-specific services, x, xii, 28, 39
general equivalency diploma (GED), 13, 14, 35
girls and female juvenile offenders, 37

H

hepatitis, 12
high school dropout, 35
HIV, 12, 13

I

incorrigibility, 19, 21, 28
institutional standards, 16

J

juvenile courts, 24, 25
juvenile crime, 27
juvenile female arrest, 24
juvenile female violent crime, 40
Juvenile Justice and Delinquency Prevention (JJDP), 22, 24, 27, 28, 31, 32, 39, 45, 46, 58, 59
Juvenile Justice and Delinquency Prevention Act, 27, 28
juvenile justice system, xii, 19, 22, 26-31, 34, 36, 37, 39, 40, 46
juvenile victimization prevention programs, xiv, 65

Index

juvenile victimization, xiv, 50

L

larceny, xii, 1, 2, 10, 12
Law Enforcement Assistance Administration (LEAA), ix, x, xi, 1, 2, 20, 21, 43, 52, 67
LEAA Task Force, ix, x, xi, 1, 20, 21, 43
low or damaged self-esteem, 35

M

male inmates, xiv, 10, 13, 15, 61
male-dominated professions, 82
maximum-security prisons, 76
mentally retarded, 27
Mothers With Infants Together (MINT), 16

N

National Advisory Commission on Criminal Justice, 16
National Crime Panel Survey, 45
National Crime Victimization Survey, 45, 54
National Institute of Corrections (NIC), viii, 8, 75, 76, 80
National Institute of Justice (NIJ), vii, 3, 8, 10, 16, 31, 51-53, 57, 60, 70
National Organization for Victim Assistance (NOVA), 43, 48, 57
National Organization for Women Legal Defense Fund, 6
National Victim Center (NVC), 45, 48, 55, 63, 64

O

Office for Victims of Crime (OVC), viii, 44, 47, 48, 56-58, 63, 64

Office of Justice Programs (OJP), vii, x, 18, 21, 41, 44, 50, 65, 67, 82, 83
Office of Juvenile Justice and Delinquency Prevention (OJJDP), 20, 27-29, 38, 45, 46
OJP Coordination Group on Women, vii, x

P

parenting programs, 16, 18
parenting skills training, xii
physical and sexual abuse, 18, 19, 31
posttraumatic stress disorder, 12
pregnancy, 7, 15, 29, 32-35, 38, 39
pregnant and parenting girls, 39
pregnant offenders, 16
prevention and treatment of juvenile delinquency, 28
progressive treatment, 29
property crimes, ix, 7
prostitution, xii, 1, 2, 10, 12, 31, 61
psychiatric morbidity, 12
public juvenile detention centers, 21

R

rehabilitative opportunities, 29
residential substance abuse treatment programs, 32
robbery, 12, 45

S

school dropout, 22, 29, 32
sexual assault treatment centers, xiii, 43, 65
sexual assault, xii, xiii, 9, 44, 48, 50, 54, 55, 56, 62, 65
sexual delinquency, 21, 28
sexual exploitation, xii
sexual harassment in the workplace, 82
sexual harassment, xv, 67, 76-80

sexually abused female, 31
Spouse Assault Replication Program (SARP), 52
stalking, xiii, 50, 57, 62
state corrections systems, 76
state planning agency (SPA), 20
substance abuse treatment, xii, 18
substance abuse, xii, 8, 10, 12, 16, 17, 18, 30, 31, 35

T

teen pregnancy and parenthood, 35
teenage pregnanc(y)ies, 16, 32, 34
truancy and school dropout, 35
truancy, 21, 28, 29, 35
tuberculosis (TB), 12, 13

U

U.S. criminal justice system, 1
U.S. Department of Justice, vii, xi, xiii, 1-3, 5, 8, 10-13, 15, 20, 44, 47, 50, 53, 54, 56-59, 61, 63, 64, 67-69, 83

V

Victim and Witness Protection Act, 46
Victims of Crime Act (VOCA), 44, 46, 48, 57
victims of stalking, 44
Victims' Rights and Restitution Act, 46
Violence Against Women Act (VAWA), xiii, 44, 46, 48, 62, 65
violence against women and girls, xiii
Violence Against Women Grants Office (VAWGO), 44, 46
Violence Against Women Office (VAWO), 46
violence against women, xiii, 50, 52, 54, 62, 65, 66

Y

young women, 19, 30-32, 34, 38, 41